Broadsides

In the War of Ideas

A Collection of Observations

Edward Cline

Patrick Henry Press

Library of Congress Cataloguing-in-Publication Data

Edward Cline (1946 -)
Broadsides in the War of Ideas/Edward Cline

ISBN-13: 978-1481800792

Cover Illustration: "U.S.S. Constitution and H.M.S. Guerriére, 19 August 1812," by Michel Felice Corne

Back Cover: Portrait of the author by Roxanne Albertoli

Patrick Henry Press
Williamsburg, VA

Publisher's Note: This book is a collection of essays published on Rule of Reason, blog site for the Center for the Advancement of Capitalism, and in other venues. These essays are copyrighted by the author.

Table of Contents

CULTURE

"You may fire when you are ready, Gridley,"
— Admiral George Dewey to Captain Charles Vernon
Gridley of the flagship *Olympia*, the Battle of Manila Bay
May 1898. Spanish-American War.

Foreword

When the U.S. went to war with Spain to enforce the Monroe Doctrine, it did not fool around. The Spanish Atlantic and Pacific Squadrons were completely destroyed. "Don't cheer, boys, the poor devils are dying," shouted Captain John Woodward Philip, of the U.S. battleship *Texas*, during the Battle of Santiago Bay, Cuba, July 1898, of Spanish sailors aboard their burning vessels or in the water swimming for their lives.

I am naturally reluctant to check my enthusiasm for the defeats or demises of the devils I assault in this volume of commentaries and essays. The initial success of *Running Out My Guns* prompted me to collect into another volume a further batch of my commentaries and essays. There are plenty more where these came from, for they represent over two decades of shouting in the wind, or raising the alarm, or emulating Paul Revere on the steed of freedom of speech: "To Arms! To Arms! The Socialists are coming! The Looters are coming! Islam is coming! The Nihilists are coming!" There is a certain pleasure to be had from raking the hull, masts, rigging and crew of an enemy warship with the best gunnery at hand, to disable the vessel and see it sink.

Again, this volume of "observations" represents a small fraction of my nonfiction efforts over the last twenty years, and focuses chiefly on what I have produced and seen published in one form or another since 2001. Most of these pieces appeared originally on Rule of Reason, the blog site of The Center for the Advancement of Capitalism, and later on, on The Dougout and Family Security Matters. They have been picked up by or linked to numerous other Internet venues, here and abroad.

And now that Congress has passed legislation which could arguably quash all such speech and mandate commensurate punishment, and now also that our government may deem all such freedom of speech as an incitement to "violence," together with the exacerbating and infuriating fact that all blog sites are now being monitored by the Department of Homeland Security (how Nazi-sounding that name is!) in search of "violence-provoking" statements made by bloggers or their readers, it is imperative that these commentaries be broadcast in the widest possible manner. We have not yet "Progressed" (as in Progressive ideology) to book-burnings or an American *Kristallnacht*, but we are inching towards it – by default, a default sired by ignorance, practiced and pragmatic evasion, and a pronounced hostility to freedom.

Long Live Lady Liberty.

Edward Cline
Williamsburg, Virgin
January 2012

Politics

Neville Chamberlain Redux

"The world must be made safe for democracy," said President Woodrow Wilson to Congress on April 2nd, 1917, some months after he proposed "peace without victory." Four days later Congress approved a declaration of war against Germany. Wilson could have asked for a declaration much earlier. German submarines were sinking neutral American shipping in a policy of unrestricted submarine warfare, five merchant ships being sunk in February and March that year alone.

Wilson had been waiting for a more "overt" act of belligerence against the U.S other than the loss of American lives at sea at German hands. But the most recent sinkings, together with the Zimmermann note to the German minister in Mexico, forced him to face reality. The Zimmermann note pledged Germany to support Mexico in an invasion of the U.S. southwest to deter certain American entry into the European conflict until after Germany had beaten Britain and France to exhaustion. If the U.S. declared war, German foreign minister Alfred Zimmermann instructed his minister in Mexico to assure Mexico that "we shall make war together and together make peace. We shall give generous financial support and it is understood that Mexico is to reconquer the lost territory in New Mexico, Texas and Arizona."

A declaration of war was not what Wilson had in mind as an altruist "tonic of a moral adventure," as editor and fellow Progressive Herbert Croly had prescribed for America years before. Rather, it was the role of mediator and "peace maker" in the conflicts and international disputes of the early 20th century.

Shuttle ahead ninety years to Georgetown University, where British Prime Minister Tony Blair, in remarks about the "new" global politics, proclaimed, "Idealism becomes the realpolitik." An essential part of that "idealism" is the introduction of "democracy" in regions of the world that have seen no legitimate governments in over a century, chiefly because their inhabitants did not know what to do with democracy, except to vote themselves new tyrants or tolerate old ones. Democracy, however, means mob rule, no matter how legitimate it sounds. It recognizes no individual rights that a majority cannot abridge or abrogate.

Even Wilson's contemporary, Vladimir Lenin, understood that. "Democracy is not identical with majority rule." Off by one adverb in that statement, he elucidates the point in contradiction of himself. "Democracy is a State which recognizes the subjection of the minority to the majority, that is, an organization for the systematic use of force by one class against the other, by one part of the population against another." (Chapter 4, *State and Revolution*, 1919)

Which is why democracy was as much his enemy as "capitalistic" republicanism, to be ruthlessly crushed. After all, in terms of a nation's population, a totalitarian party's members are always in the minority.

The point here is that President Bush's and Mr. Blair's "idealism" does not fundamentally differ from Wilson's. Its moral core consists of blind duty and the sacrifice of wealth and of lives to accomplish the spread of democracy. Integral to the concept is that the U.S. should eschew its selfish isolationism and adopt a proactive, Kantian "moral" role to correct wrongs wherever it might see them. Our political leaders are ruled by the little Prussian's categorical imperative to "do the right thing" regardless of cost, self-interest, or even of consequence.

"Democracy," rather than being an object of populist appeal or simply because it is easier for politicians to pronounce than "constitutional republic" (which is what the U.S. is becoming less and less), thus complements such "idealist realpolitik." That is the true character of Mr. Blair's "realpolitik." It is the "idealism" of humility, retreat, and ultimate self-destruction.

In the conflict with Iran and its neo-Hitlerian President Mahmoud Ahmadinejad, Bush contends that the issue of Iran's nuclear weapons development can be resolved with "robust diplomacy." That was Wilson's premise behind his proposal for an international peace conference to end the fighting between the European powers, and the basis of Neville Chamberlain's negotiations with Nazi Germany.

Wilson also said, in April 1915, that "No nation is fit to sit in judgment upon any other nation." Both Bush and Blair have refined that idea, alleging that no religion is fit to sit in judgment of any other creed. Their altruist, Christian premises forbid them to condemn Islam, and allow them to claim that Islam is not the motivating force behind terrorism. It has been "hijacked," or "perverted."

Anyone who has read the *Koran* knows this is an absurd notion, as absurd a notion that Hitler "hijacked" Nazism or that Stalin "perverted" communism. But, then, Bush and Blair believe in democracy, as well.

Some commentators may suspect that the May 31st news that the U.S. is willing to negotiate directly with Iran is a ruse to assure world opinion that it is not trying to bully Iran into giving up its nuclear enrichment program, and that it does not intend to employ force against Iran.

Given recent developments, we can believe that it is not a ruse. President Bush and Secretary of State Condoleezza Rice are willing to take both of Ahmadinejad's hands and personally lead him to the higher plateau of international amity, global peace, and pure "democracy," with Prime Minister Blair, Europe, Russia, China and others flinging confetti and flowers at them. Ahmadinejad can snarl and missile-rattle all he wishes; Bush and Rice are willing to forget dignity and take the abuse in the name of a higher cause.

Ahmadinejad is a beast, they agree. But he is there, a metaphysical given, and must be dealt with without igniting more conflict or exacerbating existing animosity. Ma Rice acknowledges that Iran is a supporter of terrorism "in Lebanon and Palestinian territories," she remarked at a news conference, according to an Associated Press report on May 31st. But, "Iran can and should be a responsible state." No mention by her or Bush of its support of terrorism in Iraq, where Iran's "insurgent" proxies and planners are picking off Americans and Iraqis by the busload. Apparently, that is not "overt' enough an act of war.

Nazi Germany and Imperial Japan were also metaphysical givens. Our policy more than half a century ago was to erase those givens, and that was the end of that. There were no negotiating "tables" to lure dictators to in the name of peace, just the burnt out shell of the Reichstag and the wind-blown ashes of Hiroshima.

As [the late] John David Lewis, a professor of classics at Ashland University, remarked in correspondence elsewhere in response to the AP report, "Note that Rice's admission that Iran has a right to nuclear energy is the same error the British made prior to

3

WW II, when they accepted that Germany had the same 'right to self-determination' as other nations."

Iran's "self-determination," in light of its record and especially in view of Ahmadinejad's bellicose rantings, includes the "destiny" of ruling the Mideast by force or subversion, the annihilation of Israel, and setting the terms of peace with the rest of the world in a quest for a *Pax Persia* via nuclear payload.

In the staring contest between Ahmadinejad, Bush and Rice, the pragmatists blinked. So they must always blink when facing bellicosity. Their concept of ensuring national security is to offer the aggressor bribes, such as the U.S and Britain did in Vienna on June 1st, and to rule out military force.

The "realpolitik" of U.S. policy to date has been one of uncompromising pragmatism. Pragmatism as an "ideal" and as a policy must by its nature sacrifice the good to evil; otherwise it would not be pragmatism. Evil derives its strength from compromised and ultimately vanquished principles. Pragmatism discounts principles as a guide to moral conduct; they are forgotten in a rush to keep a nemesis at bay.

The principle left behind here is the right of the U.S. to its self-defense against a threatening rogue state. Reason and reality have no role in a policy of pragmatism. Yet, despite pragmatism's sorry and costly role in history, especially in the 20th century, current leaders are convinced that pragmatism is the only "moral" path to follow. They are determined to make it "work." But it works only to the benefit of the enemies of civilization.

The New York Times, under the chortling headline on June 1st, "Bush's Realization on Iran: No Good Choice Left Except Talk," reported that the president asked Rice "several months ago that he needed 'a third option,' a way to get beyond either a nuclear Iran or an American military action." The term "beyond" is eloquently appropriate; it suggests an excursion into fantasyland in search of a Star Trekian "Prime Directive." Bush has explicitly rejected an "either/or" in favor of an evasive, non-confrontational middle course.

One must wonder about the psychology of men who are so afraid of absolutes that they are willing to acknowledge a threat but never the rational course of action to take to remove one. According to the AP report, when Rice was asked about the possibility of the U.S. reestablishing diplomatic relations with Iran, Rice "ruled out a 'grand bargain.' However, she said a negotiated solution to the nuclear dispute could 'begin to change the relationship.'"

"Nobody is confused about the nature of this regime," said Rice at a news conference held to announce the alleged shift in policy. "We are not negotiating the terms of terrorism."

Were she and Bush genuinely confused about the nature of Iran's regime, it might be forgivable. But she names what she and Bush both know, and that makes the action an unforgivable betrayal. In effect, their willingness to "come to the table" to talk is, in effect, a willingness to negotiate the terms of terrorism.

Is it any wonder that Ahmadinejad is so contemptuously confident that Islam will triumph? Even psychopaths like him can sense cowardice and smell blood. Ahmadinejad has mastered Hitler's playbook of the 1930's.

The overture to the U.S.'s creeping, inevitable capitulation on Iran was reported in the *Los Angeles Times* of May 26th under the appropriate headline, "The Tyranny Doctrine."

"Last week, Secretary of State...Rice announced resumption of full U.S. diplomatic relations with Libya, citing Tripoli's renunciation of terrorism and intelligence cooperation." The article asserts that this move "marks an effective end to the Bush doctrine."

Rather, it highlights a continuation of the Bush doctrine of non-judgmental pragmatism, which has been to take the path of least resistance and greatest expediency, to avoid confronting major threats and to expend lives and treasure on incidentals, such as Iraq and Afghanistan. Not to mention, in this instance, a forgiving of Libyan dictator Qadhaffi for the murder of hundreds of Westerners by his own army of jihadists. There is "realpolitik" for you.

The Los Angeles Times article goes on to list Bush's record of non-achievements in his pursuit of global "democracy":

> "The Bush administration has watched Egypt abrogate elections, ignored the collapse of the so-called Cedar Revolution in Lebanon and abandoned Chinese dissidents; now Washington is mulling a peace treaty with Stalinist North Korea."

The mare's nest of pragmatism and its consequences grows nastier, thicker and more perilous. When will Bush have his own "reality check" and grasp the true nature of our enemies? When we experience another September 11th?

Bush, at his second inauguration, stated: "The survival of liberty in our land increasingly depends on the success of liberty in other lands. The best hope for peace in our world is the expansion of freedom in all the world." The first half of this statement is not strictly true; liberty in America can succeed without it succeeding elsewhere in the world. But what if the rest of the world rejects the peace that freedom can bring, and chooses the "peace" of submission, tyranny or conquest?

The world, indeed, is being made safe, but not for freedom.

June 2006

Clueless George

It is a double measure of today's bottomless political ignorance and of the intellectual gulf that separates our first chief executives from modern ones that anyone could thoughtlessly compare the purpose of the American Revolution with the aims of the "war on terror." On February 19th, President George Bush visited Mount Vernon on the occasion of George Washington's 275th birthday. He exemplified such a measure in what he said.

"Today, we're fighting a new war to defend our liberty and our people and our way of life," Bush said in a speech at Mount Vernon. "And as we work to advance the cause of freedom around the world, we remember that the father of our country boasted that the freedoms we secured in our revolution were not meant for Americans alone."

Without stooping to dwell much on George Bush's composition skills or his knowledge of history, I am sure he did not write his own speech, and equally certain that much of what he said in it about George Washington was new to him. One of the tasks of speechwriters is to imbue the office of President with a façade of wisdom and literacy. I am willing to bet that Bush, until he vetted the speech, did not know that many new Americans clamored for Washington to become King George the First of the United States, demonstrating even then the vestiges of a clinging psychological need for a monarch.

Many things in Bush's speech offended me. I will begin with the paragraph quoted above.

> "Today, we're fighting a new war to defend our liberty and our people and our way of life."

No, we are not. We are expending lives and treasure in an altruist moral adventure to spread "democracy" in Islamic countries, something neither George Washington nor any of his immediate successors in office could not conceive of doing. Our liberty, such as is left of it in our declining *republic*, is not being "defended," but rather is being sacrificed and discarded in ever growing chunks to the welfare state. And "our people" can be best defended, and the security of this country ensured, by adopting a policy Bush has evaded ever since 9/11: by removing the Islamic threat, and leaving the Muslims to their own devices.

Our "way of life"? I do not know what this phrase means any more. It cannot mean freedom that is protected by the government, because our government is the worst violator of our freedoms. More and more, Americans are expected to report or account to the government in virtually every aspect of their lives. Remember, for example, that April 15th is approaching, and that Americans now work nearly half a year for the federal government to pay income taxes.

> "And as we work to advance the cause of freedom around the world, we remember that the father of our country boasted that the freedoms we secured in our revolution were not meant for Americans alone."

It is not this country's "duty" to educate at its own expense and the price of American lives other countries on the morality and practicality of freedom. But, how can we work to advance the "cause of freedom" when we have forgotten what "freedom" is, or what are its roots or cause, or never knew freedom except for the crumbs of it that have fallen from the banquet table of statist largess, ultimately destined to be swept up by the federal wait staff? How can we advance it in countries whose citizens do not want it, but "democratically" prefer to structure their lives around a religious book of abominable irrationality (e.g., the *Bible*, or the *Koran*)?

How many our soldiers in Iraq or Afghanistan will admit before a television news camera that they don't believe they are fighting for Iraqi or Afghani freedom at all, but rather for the "freedom" of men to flagellate themselves with swords and chains and to compel women to behave like two-legged chattel sheathed in black winding sheets? None. If those soldiers are under the gun of correctness or orders, they'll say what they are expected to say to save themselves certain grief meted out by their politically correct commanders.

Elsewhere in his speech, Bush stated:

> "When the American people chose Washington for the role [of president], he reluctantly accepted....Washington accepted the presidency because the office needed him, not because he needed the office."

While it is true that Washington preferred to remain a private citizen, Bush's assertion suggests that Washington was solely motivated by a sense of self-sacrifice, which is perfectly in conformance with Bush's own code of altruism. While I am not a Washington scholar, I know enough about the man that it is more likely he accepted the presidency because the nation he had fought to create was a value to him. The lesser value to him was his status of a private citizen safely ensconced at Mount Vernon. What would that relative serenity have meant to him if he saw that nation on the brink of dissolution and anarchy?

Washington's honesty and courage have become the stuff of legend. Children are taught to revere his name, and leaders look to him for strength in uncertain times."

Where anymore are "children taught to revere his name"? How many of them go on to college perhaps never having encountered Washington in their "social studies," or think that he was president during the Civil War? And if, by chance, they are expected by teachers to "revere" his name, in today's multiculturalist, would they have been instructed to share that reverence with the likes of Robert Mugabe or Mao or Mahatma Gandhi?

And what "strength" could modern American leaders derive from Washington's example when they hold that uncertainty, pragmatism and expediency are the bywords of foreign and domestic policies? Washington's character, integrity, and stature can be only unreal or invisible to modern politicians.

Washington was neither an intellectual giant nor a political philosopher. Neither is George W. Bush. But, picturing them standing side-by-side produces an incredible incongruity. In every respect by which we can judge men, it is a pygmy versus a giant.

One wonders what passed through George Bush's mind as he spoke about Washington on February 19th. I can only paraphrase a line from *Book*

Four: Empire, from *Sparrowhawk*, in which another little man incurs the anger the giant:

> "As he spoke, he could only imagine the ludicrousness of his small frame standing toe to toe in opposition to the towering figure of George Washington."

February 2007

Rivals for Your Life: Religious Conservatives vs. Islam

"If you, as a servant of your god, must use one hundred thousand warriors to destroy me, a solitary servant of my God, then you whisper to *me*, Muhammed Ahmed, who will be remembered from Khartoum: your god or mine?"

— General Charles Gordon to the Mahdi in *Khartoum* (1966). Writer, Robert Ardey

In April 2009 I noted in a column, "The Irrelevancy of Conservatism," which was devoted to examining why conservatives and the Left hated novelist-philosopher Ayn Rand, that

> Rand herself marked the malaise of conservatism in 1962 in her essay, "Conservatism: An Obituary." Identifying why conservatism was finished as a distinct political ideology and political force, she wrote:

> *"If the 'conservatives' do not stand for capitalism, they stand for and are nothing; they have no goal, no direction, no political principles, no social ideals, no intellectual values, no leadership to offer anyone. Yet capitalism is what the 'conservatives' dare not advocate or defend. They are paralyzed by the profound conflict between capitalism and the moral code which dominates our culture: altruism."*

> More importantly, however, the article reveals that conservatives are afraid that men are realizing that Ayn Rand is fundamentally relevant to today's political, moral and economic crises, and that they, the conservatives, have grown irrelevant. The "transcendent order" of Russell Kirk (1918-1994), cited by [William R.] Hawkins as a source of moral and political wisdom, was based "variously on tradition, divine revelation, or natural law," but has made way for the "transcendent order" of the brute collectivism of the state, to which Americans are more and more expected to defer.

> *"What should really agitate the public is not the principle of government intervention to prevent an economic*

10

collapse, but how the politicians have seized the opportunity
to spend huge sums on non-emergency, special interest
programs."

And what is the wisdom of conservatives? It is the "dean of
conservative thinking" Russell Kirk's, which the reader may sample
here, beginning with:

> "....Conservatism is the negation of ideology: it is a state of
> mind, a type of character, a way of looking at the civil social
> order."

So it is an anti-ideology, or a set of "sentiments" and non-ideas,
or a "state of mind" which is supposed to animate anyone to try to
dam the advancing, liberty-destroying lava of statism. Hawkins
offers his conservative credentials in this outburst:

> "The most alarming sign that the anarchists are trying to take
> over the Tea Party movement is the sudden revival of the
> amoral and anti-social screeds of the late and unlamented
> Ayn Rand. Her name has been bantered around far too often
> on talk radio and by Fox News commentators."

Hawkins should wonder why her name is so frequently
"bantered around," and not [William F.] Buckley's or Russell Kirk's.
Perhaps it is because men are searching for answers and ideas, Rand
has had them for decades, and answers and ideas are not to be found
in conservatism. He should also learn that Rand was neither an
anarchist nor a libertarian.

As if to underscore the religious, anti-reason color of
conservatism, Hawkins manages to introduce Original Sin as an
ingredient of the financial crisis:

> "True conservatives know the character of Mankind is
> 'fallen' and that there is a dark side to human nature to
> which bankers and fund managers are just as vulnerable as
> anyone else. Freedom without responsibility, and rights
> without duties, leads to license and wrong-doing."

I ask here, almost three years later: What responsibilities? What
duties? Hawkins names none. And why are rights contingent on
meeting and fulfilling them? True conservatives, however, speak for
themselves. Only they know how far they have "fallen" and are more

acquainted with the dark side of their "souls" than they should wish anyone else to be.

Premises have a way of percolating to the top sooner or later. This is the case with conservatism, specifically religious conservatism. There is secular conservatism, which is more a species of pragmatism than it is of principled ideology. Capitalism "works." A modicum of freedom "works." (But not "too much" of either.) And there is religious conservatism, which is a marriage of pragmatism and faith, otherwise known as "social conservatism."

Republican Presidential candidate Rick Santorum gave us an idea of what it means to be a "social conservative." The Blaze offers the low-down on Santorum and explodes the notion that he is against "big government."

Today, Santorum tells voters that Medicare is "crushing" the "entire health care system." In 2003, Santorum voted for the Medicare drug entitlement that costs taxpayers more than $60 billion a year and almost $16 trillion in unfunded liabilities. Santorum voted for the 2005 "bridge to nowhere" bill and was an earmark enthusiast his entire career.

> These days, Santorum regularly joins a chorus of voices claiming that he would greatly reduce the role of federal government in local education. When he had a say, he supported No Child Left Behind and expanded the federal control of school systems. In his book, in fact, Santorum advocates dictating a certain curriculum to all schools. The right kind. *It's not the authority of government that irks him, but rather the content of the material Washington is peddling today.* [*Italics* mine.]

There is no reason that candidate Mitt Romney is any different. He's a social conservative, too. What is it that social conservatives want to "conserve"? "Traditional" values and big government as our shepherd and arbiter of those values. Hardly an ideology.

The fundamental obstacle for conservatives to understanding the pernicious influence of altruism is precisely their altruist premises. They will not question those premises. To question them is to question the role of government as a proactive agent for altruism as an apology for freedom and capitalism. The history of conservatism, especially in the 20th century, bears out the truth of this contention.

The Left allies itself with Islam because of shared totalitarian yearnings and ends.

Religious conservatives, however, oppose Islam basically because it is a rival creed, a "competing faith." It is not a turn-the-other-cheek creed. It advocates throwing stones, lots of stones, in the form of real rocks and passenger jets and arsonist's torches. The quotation from *Khartoum* that precedes this column may be taken as evidence of that fear, although Charlton Heston's Gordon, speaking with conviction to Laurence Olivier as the Mahdi, doesn't seem particularly fearful. But after his first fictive meeting with the Mahdi, he confesses to an aide:

> "I seem to have suffered the illusion that I have a monopoly on God."

Perhaps that's why conservatives hate Islam. Let's look at the "Five Pillars of Islam":

> Allah is the only God and Mohammad his prophet (*shahada*)
> The Haj (or pilgrimage to Mecca)
> Prayer five times a day (*sala*)
> The giving of alms (*zaka*)
> Ramadan (*saum*, month-long fasting)

We are all now familiar with the unnamed "sixth" pillar of Islam: *Jihad*.

What are the parallel pillars of the Christian faith? The Christian God is the only God. To some Christians, Allah is an apostate, or Satan himself; to others, he's just another "false idol" with peculiar habits. A one-time trip to Vatican City to hear the Pope give his Easter sermon can be taken as the Christian Haj. I don't think other Christian denominations have a similar obligatory pilgrimage to make. Prayer five times a day isn't required of Christians, although I'm certain many pray every day before meals and participating in sports events and the like. Charity is also a major altruistic practice in Christianity; in fact, it's regarded as a key virtue. Lent is the Christian Ramadan.

Jihad? The only modern equivalents have been the missionary "outreaches" of the 19th and early 20th centuries, and the modern versions. These, however, have never entailed violence against pagans or infidels or native populations. The Spaniards, however, took along priests to convert South American Indians to Christianity as sanctifying baggage in their quest for gold, and there were the religious wars of Europe.

So, the similarities are there. An interesting site, "Theological differences between Islam and Christianity," features a *précis* on the doctrinal differences between Christianity, Judaism, and Islam:

> The faith of Muslims is based on the works of accomplishing the five pillars of Islam. Christianity, on the contrary, it based on faith that people can be freed from their sin[s] by the blood of Christ Jesus.

Most Arabs are Muslim, but most Muslims are not Arabs. There are millions of followers who are of Persian and Asian descent. Arabs came from the line of Ishmael (the half brother of Isaac - father of the Jews). However, descendants of Ishmael were a nomadic people who intermarried with the Midianites (*Judges* 8:1, 12, 22, 24) and others, while the Hebrews largely avoided a racial mix. After Islam violently imposed its doctrines on the Arab world, Muslim men were permitted to take wives of any faith in order to raise the children in Islam. (Muslim women were [and still are] obligated to marry only Muslim men.)

Those who practice the "Five Pillars" of Islam worship a god named Allah, who was the chief god of the Quraish tribe that controlled Mecca. This god was selected by Mohammad from among the 300 plus idols honored at the Ka'aba, and Muhammed tried to modify his moon god to become the God of Abraham. The symbol of this moon god, Allah, is known as the crescent symbol of Islam. Conversely, the Christian god revealed Himself to Moses as "Yahweh" (*Exodus* 3:14-16). In the Torah and in the Koran, Allah and Yahweh speak in the third person plural, yet both Judaism and Islam dogmatically proclaim their god to be singular. ("Hear Oh Israel, the Lord your God is One God" *Deut.* 6:4) As Christianity branched off of Judaism, they saw this as additional evidence for the Trinity.

All varieties of Christianity are founded on saving one's soul, or on personal salvation, and the different denominations encourage or prescribe various degrees of ardor to that end. This does not necessarily entail, either, going on a homicidal rampage.

> Christianity, on the other hand, follows the Lord God of Israel. Christians believe that God sent His Son to Earth to be the atonement for sin....[A]ll a person needs to do is accept the forgiveness of Jesus Christ. The Great Commission to all Christians states, "Go therefore and make

disciples of all the nations, baptizing them in the name of the Father and of the Son and of the Holy Spirit, teaching them to observe all things that I have commanded you; and lo, I am with you always, even to the end of the age." *Matthew* 28:18-20, NKJV.

Personal salvation in Islam, however, is as bloody-minded as one can imagine.

Muhammed specified that God does not have a son. Because of this, there is no redemption from sin in Islam. Salvation comes by works which never carry an assurance of being good enough unless one were to die for Allah as a suicide bomber or die killing infidels in battle. "If you should die or be killed in the cause of Allah, His mercy and forgiveness would surely be better than all they riches they amass. If you should die or be killed, before Him you shall all be gathered" (*Sura* 3:157-8). "Those who are slain in the way of Allah - he will never let their deeds be lost. Soon will he guide them and improve their condition, and admit them to the Garden, which he has announced for them" (*Sura* 47:5).

Another religious site, "Yahweh (the God of the Bible) vs. Allah (the god of the Koran)," stresses these differences between Christianity and Islam (comments in brackets are mine):

(A) Allah is distant and unknowable. The God of the Bible is close and personal.

(B) Allah does not love every person; Yahweh [God's moniker in the Old Testament] does love every person. [Although he did have his temper tantrums and could be maliciously capricious, causing plagues of locusts, deaths of first-borns, turning wives into pillars of salt, the Tower of Babble, and so on. This is the "tough love" of a psychotic, and differs little from Allah's behavior.]

(C) Allah did not, would not, and will not die for you, nor would he ever send anyone to do so [Allah did not have a son]. But the God of the Bible loves you so much He sent His one and only Son to die for you. And He stands ready to grant you everlasting life if you will receive Him by faith. [Islam, or "submission," by any other name.]

Both Christian conservatives in America and Islamic fundamentalists seem to hate gays, hold traditionally non-Progressive old school conservative ideologies, demean women, and are guided in their lifestyle and thinking by their basic doctrinal texts, i.e., the Bible and Koran. Which, condensed, means adhering to an old time religion, because it requires nothing more than faith and credulity.

We can understand the animosity held by Islam for Christianity. The Koran is very clear about what to do about the "People of the Book" – slay, subjugate, or convert them if they don't accept the Koran as God's final word and Mohammad as the last and most important prophet. Islam is the youngest of the three major faiths and much of its doctrine was cadged from Christian and Jewish scripture – with much tongue-in-cheek inventiveness over the centuries. And Islam does not so much fear Christianity as hates it and intends to eradicate it.

But why do especially Christian conservatives hate and fear Islam? When one reads the comments on the latest Islamic depredation or instance of *taqiyya* on sites such as Jihad Watch or Atlas Shrugs, a fair percentage of the readers feel obligated to bring God into the discussion. Their ardor is virtually palpable, and any deprecatory remark made by an atheist about Christianity or God usually provokes outrage and posses form. There is a clinical or sociological term for such mob behavior: majority syncing bias.

Because most of Christian doctrine is founded on the life, homilies, and travails of Jesus Christ, possibly that fear and hatred of Islam are based on the secondary status that Islam accords Christ, as a mere prophet, not a "son of God." Islam claims he was sent to earth by Allah to advance the cause of Islam. In fact, Islam contends that Christ was never crucified, but simply "raised up to Him."

"Islam and the People of the Book," by Anwar Shaikh, provides a very simple explanation that supports this contention:

> Of course, the Koran treats Jesus as a Prophet of God and confirms that he had been given the power to perform miracles but it defies the Christian fundamentals. For example, it refutes the doctrine of Crucifixion, which holds that God made His Son the Sacrificial Lamb to carry away the people's burdens of sin:

"...for their saying, We slew the Messiah, Jesus son of Mary, the Messenger of God. Yet they did not slay him, neither crucified him, only a likeness of that was shown them... God raised him up to Him..." (IV - *Women*: 155)

It means that God did not allow Jesus to suffer crucifixion, which is the kernel of the Christian faith. He raised him from the cross, and replaced him with someone, who looked like Jesus. Thus Islam destroys the very foundation of Christianity. Not only that, Islam subordinates Jesus to Muhammad. The Hadith No. 287 of Sahih Muslim, volume one, states: "...the son of Mary will soon descend among you as a just judge. He will break crosses, kill swine and abolish Jizya..."

That is, Christ will return to destroy Christianity at Allah's behest. Presumably Judaism and Jews will have been exterminated long before Christ reappears. Muslim Brotherhood Legal Expert Yusuf al Qaradawi earnestly wishes it to happen. He's President Obama's pick to negotiate a "peace" between the U.S. and the Taliban. In 2009, on Al-Jazeera, he implored:

"Throughout history, Allah has imposed upon the [Jews] people who would punish them for their corruption. The last punishment was carried out by Hitler. By means of all the things he did to them–even though they exaggerated this issue–he managed to put them in their place. This was divine punishment for them. Allah willing, the next time will be at the hand of the believers."

It's all part of Allah's plan, don't you know. Christ, however, is noted for wanting to be kind to animals. Would the Islamic Christ approve of *halal*, and really go about killing swine? And dogs? And apes?

And Christianity and Islam both have their unique versions of the "end of days." The sun will rise in the West, billions of corpses will come back to life, stars will go out or fall to earth, the Horsehead Nebula will neigh, the Crab Nebula will sidle up to Orion, almost knocking over the Pillars of Creation, there will be earthquakes and pestilence, water running up hill, and everyone queuing up in an infinite line to be judged by one or the other deity (you *can* make this stuff up; the Bible, the Koran, the Torah, and other religious documents prove it). St. Peter and God are on one side of this vast celestial arena, the Angel Gabriel and Allah on the other, ready with their naughty-nice lists. Satan and his legions of minions are waiting and fuming (literally, they're from Hades) outside the arena, impatient to collect kindling for the hellfire as Allah or God casts souls into it.

What a premise for an *opera bouffe*!

There are no serious or fundamental conflicts between men of reason. Reason is their guide. If there are conflicts or differences between them, the most consistent man will be proven right. Knowable reality will govern the outcome. But conflicts between mere beliefs – beliefs without evidence of what is believed, beliefs based on the unknowable, beliefs based on the whim or emotion that "I just want it to be so" – have led and will continue to lead to horrific warfare in which force determines the victor and the outcome without really settling the question of whose God was greater.

God, after all, has always been on the side of enemy combatants.

Islam is not only a major rival religion to Christianity, but it also has an aura of greater potency which Christian conservatives must envy. It sanctions violence and deceit as Christianity does not, and flouts practically all of the Ten Commandments.

Violence and deceit are great time-savers when one is trying to collect souls and extort *jizya* from the greatest number for the greater God in the shortest time. Thus, failing persuasion or *dawa*, Islam can just barge into societies and cultures and nations with sword and club and impose its will, committing murder, coveting and taking wives and property, lying from ear to ear, cursing, taking the name of the other guy's God in vain, sparing those who recognize Allah, and so on.

Of course, in Islam, everything a person does is "written," predestined to happen by Allah. So the average Muslim is but an automaton. He's only doing what Allah intended him to do. Still, if he slays unbelievers and other infidels and is killed "in action," as a "martyr," he will be guaranteed Paradise. So, Islamic justice is hard to reconcile with reason. One may as well pat one's coffee-maker on the head for, well, making coffee, and tie a bright red ribbon around it.

But then Christian ethics is little better. Without going into the issue of the contradictory attributes of omniscience and omnipotence – some Christian doctrines allege that God also knew everything that one will do eons before one's Stone Age great-great-grandparents were conceived – one encounters the minimal role of volition as the key to one's salvation. It also renders the deed-doer selfless, as well, because no good deed is supposed to be performed with the expectation of reward – not even personal, "spiritual" satisfaction – but only for its own sake as a Kantian maxim. Instead of performing the deed in the name of Allah, it is done in the name of the deed. The least quantum of self-interest in performing a good deed leaves the deed tainted with selfishness or with greed for absolution or a place in Heaven.

Naturally, this puts the receiver or beneficiary of a good deed in a moral quandary. It is his happiness and well-being that is supposed to be one's motive. But shouldn't the same maxim apply to the beneficiary? If his life is saved by a selfless benefactor, how can he *not* feel selfishly grateful? Ideally, he should feel just as selflessly disinterested in the preservation of his life as the benefactor was supposed to have been in having saved it.

The consistent altruist would be dead from a brief career of selfless service to others. And the consistent beneficiary would be dead from refusal to accept any alms, for they would only make him happy. So, "social conservatives" find a comfortable medium between altruism and staying alive. The policy explains their practiced compartmentalization of Christian morality, their hypocrisies and inconsistencies, and their politics.

"Ay, there's the rub," mused Hamlet. Christians consider it nobler to suffer the slings and arrows of outrageous illogic rather than acknowledge it.

Logical conundrums, however, do not weigh upon the minds of devout Muslims. Islam does not paint itself into such ethical corners. It is not concerned with contradictions, moral absurdities, or syllogistic traps. It is brutally frank in its means and ends. Convert or die, or cough up the protection money. Nice cheek, infidel Christian. Can you turn the other one? Thanks for tolerating me. Now, get out of my way.

Perhaps that is why Islam is feared – and envied – by its rival religionists. Its god was remembered. And that bothers the Christians. Look at the Sudan today. And Egypt.

The Mahdi has triumphed, after all.

January 2012

Gunboat Pragmatism

Broadcast news coverage is becoming as chummy and surfacy as "Entertainment Tonight" and "Access Hollywood." Driven by "personality" and photogenics, the kidding banter and annoying silliness of the morning and evening anchors for ABC, CBS and NBC almost makes one pine for the serious, dour days of Walter Cronkite.

Listening to the current political debates between the presidential candidates – or perhaps they should be called "personality" debates, for their political content is virtually nil – has become, to date, as deafening as a forest full of croaking tree frogs at midnight. These human tree frogs may be communicating something to each other, but not to the public's ears.

And reading about the U.S.'s efforts to bring "peace" and "stability" to the Mideast and to Iraq is akin to being sentenced to read the entire dismal oeuvre of Franz Kafka, a special edition illustrated with etchings by Edvard Munch.

Instead of acknowledging our enemies – after first identifying them – and taking the proper military actions to neutralize or destroy them to ensure this country's safety, our policy is has been to treat them all as potential or imagined allies, to deem them "forces of moderation" in the pursuit of peace and stability in the region, and to reward them with military hardware.

The most recent instance of this foolishness is the Bush administration's proposed $20 billion weapons sale to Saudi Arabia and its neighboring feudal kingdoms, tyrannies, and regimes, every one of them hostile to the U.S. and to its only regional ally, Israel.

To "balance" this the U.S. is also proposing to sell about $30 billion in slightly more advanced military hardware to Israel, a country every one of our Arab "allies" would prefer to erase from existence in the name of the same Mideast "peace" and "security."

The New York Times of July 28 reports, under the headline "U.S. Set to Offer Huge Arms Deal to Saudi Arabia":

> "The proposed package of advanced weaponry for Saudi Arabia, which includes advanced satellite-guided bombs, upgrades to its fighters and new naval vessels, has made Israel and some of its supporters in Congress nervous. Senior officials who described the package on Friday said they believed that the administration had resolved those concerns, in part by promising Israel $30.4 billion in military aid over

the next decade, a significant increase over what Israel has received in the past 10 years.

"Along with Saudi Arabia, Bahrain, Kuwait, Oman, Qatar and the United Arab Emirates are likely to receive equipment and weaponry from the arms sales under consideration, officials said. In general, the U.S. is interested in upgrading the countries' air and missile defense systems, improving their navies and making modest improvements in their air forces."

Ostensibly, all this aid is meant to "protect" these fiefdoms from Iranian military designs. And every one of those fiefdoms holds the U.S. hostage via their expropriated oil production. This would not be a problem, if the U.S. were not held hostage by environmentalists, who refuse to allow the development of known offshore oil reserves and the construction of new refineries.

The U.S. will "insist" that that the weaponry not be used against Israel. In the meantime, Iran is not acknowledged by the Bush administration as an enemy, either. Consider the contrast: When Nazi Germany invaded Poland and France, we did not send envoys to Berlin to plead for "peace" and "stability" in Europe. When we secured a defeated Germany and Italy, Britain did not accuse the U.S. of an "illegal occupation," as Saudi Arabia has publicly charged the U.S.

Perhaps the most revealing sentence in this report is:

"In talks about the package, the administration has not sought specific assurances from Saudi Arabia that it would be more supportive of the American effort in Iraq as a condition of receiving the arms package, the officials said."

That is, the U.S. will not demand that Saudi Arabia stop sending Sunni "insurgents" into Iraq to kill American troops. Also, the U.S. is "certain" that Saudi Arabia is not only financially supporting Sunni groups in Iraq, but that it is working to bring down the Shiite-dominated Iraqi government. Another

Times article from July 27, "Saudis' Role in Iraq Frustrates U.S. Officials," reports:

"...Bush administration officials are voicing increasing anger at what they say has been Saudi Arabia's counterproductive role in the Iraq war. They say that beyond regarding Mr. Maliki as an Iranian [or Shiite] agent, the Saudis have offered financial support to Sunni groups....Of an estimated 60 to 80 foreign fighters who enter Iraq each month, American military and intelligence officials say that nearly half are coming from Saudi Arabia and that the Saudis have not done enough to stem the flow."

Elsewhere in the article, the *Times* revealed:

"The American officials in Iraq also say that the majority of suicide bombers in Iraq are from Saudi Arabia and that about 40 percent of all foreign fighters are Saudi. Officials said that while most of the foreign fighters came to Iraq to become suicide bombers, others arrived as bomb makers, snipers, logisticians and financiers."

But the U.S. continues to regard Saudi Arabia as an "ally" and a "force for moderation." Franz Kafka could not have conceived of a more existentially obscene and futile a policy.

Literary lights consider Kafka's short story, "The Metamorphosis," in which a man overnight turns into an insect, as his *pièce de résistance*. "Insects" properly characterizes the formulators and purveyors of current U.S. foreign policy, and they have been insects for at least the last half-century.

Pragmatism, after all, in the name of practicality in pursuit of a "Platonic" peace, eschews making moral judgments and taking actions based on those judgments. In the run-up to the U.S. withdrawal from Iraq, pragmatism will prove to be not so "practical" after all. The current Iraqi government, created and propped up by the U.S. at the expense of American lives and treasure, on the transparent fiction that such a "stable" government will ensure America's security, will either eventually fall from Saudi efforts, or be "co-opted" by Iran (and there is evidence that this is already the case) to threaten Israel and Saudi Arabia. Iranian "fighters" are already competing with Saudi "fighters" on many American lives they can take.

In the 19th century, Western powers, including the U.S., applied a policy of "gunboat diplomacy" to protect American and Western lives and commercial interests in countries whose governments would not protect them from killers and looters. A warship need only appear in the waters outside such a country, and the crisis would be over.

Today, we are proposing to give those renegade governments the weapons with which to threaten or destroy American lives, not only in those countries, but in the U.S. itself.

Philosopher Harry Binswanger remarked recently:

> "America's security does not require that a proper government be installed in Iraq, Iran, Syria, etc. Our security requires only that the various fanatical bands in the region know full well that the moment they raise a hint of a threat to Americans, they will be crushed. We should let Baathists, Shiites, Hamas, the PLO, Al Quada, and Hezbollah all fight each other – as long as they all know they must keep clear of America....If the Arab/Muslim populations are not culturally advanced enough to embrace the institutions of a free society, that is their problem, not ours...."

I endorse that thinking one hundred percent. We should adopt Rhett Butler's attitude towards Scarlett O'Hara at the end of "Gone with the Wind": Frankly, we shouldn't give a damn whether or not they discover those institutions or continue to butcher each other in the name of a ghost. Just don't point your guns on our direction – or else.

August 2007

America Was Not Gilead

A reader queried The Center for the Advancement of Capitalism asking for sources that would substantiate the assertion in my letter to the *Wall Street Journal* ("State Department's Faith-Based Initiatives," July 31) that the U.S. was not founded on Christian principles, but secular ones. Here is my reply, and the instances cited below do not begin to exhaust the amount of proof:

From **Thomas Jefferson's** *Notes on Virginia* (1782)

"The returning good sense of our country threatens abortion to their hopes, & they [the clergy] believe that any portion of power confided to me, will be exerted in opposition to their schemes. And they believe rightly; for I have sworn upon the altar of God, eternal hostility against every form of tyranny over the mind of man. But this is all they have to fear from me: & enough too in their opinion, & this is the cause of their printing lying pamphlets against me . . ."

Jefferson endorsed individual freedom; he argued that any form of government control, not only of religion, but of individual mercantilism, was tyranny. He maintained that our rights have no dependence on our religious opinions, that is, that individual rights do not derive from religious dogma or belief, but from observable nature. Whether or not a "God" was responsible for that nature, was to him and to most of his fellow Founders, utterly irrelevant.

Also:

"Question with boldness even the existence of a god; because if there be one he must approve of the homage of reason more than that of blindfolded fear." – Letter to Peter Carr, August 10, 1787

From **James Madison**, fourth president of the U.S.:

"Every new & successful example of a perfect separation between ecclesiastical and civil matters is of importance." – Letter to Edward Livingston, July 10, 1822.

"And I have no doubt that every new example will succeed, as every past one has done, in shewing that religion & Govt will both exist in greater purity, the less they are mixed." – Letter to Edward Livingston, July 10, 1822, in Saul K. Padover, ed., *The Complete Madison: His Basic Writings* (1953).

"The civil government...functions with complete success...by the total separation of the Church from the State." – Madison, *Writings* Volume 8, p. 432, quote from Gene Garman, "Essays in Addition to *America's Real Religion.*"

From **Benjamin Franklin**:

"I have found Christian dogma unintelligible. Early in life, I absenteed myself from Christian assemblies."

"Lighthouses are more helpful then churches."

From **John Adams**:

"The question before the human race is, whether the God of nature shall govern the world by his own laws, or whether priests and kings shall rule it by fictitious miracles?" – Letter to Thomas Jefferson, June 20, 1815.

"The United States of America have exhibited, perhaps, the first example of governments erected on the simple principles of nature; and if men are now sufficiently enlightened to disabuse themselves of artifice, imposture, hypocrisy, and superstition, they will consider this event as an era in their history. Although the detail of the formation of the American governments is at present little known or regarded either in Europe or in America, it may hereafter become an object of curiosity. It will never be pretended that any persons employed in that service had interviews with the gods, or were in any degree under the influence of Heaven, more than those at work upon ships or houses, or laboring in merchandise or agriculture; it will forever be acknowledged that these governments were contrived merely by the use of reason and the senses." – Adams, "A Defence of the Constitution of Government of the United States of America" (1787-88), from Adrienne Koch, ed., *The American Enlightenment: The Shaping of the American Experiment and a Free Society* (1965), p. 258, quoted from

Ed and Michael Buckner, "Quotations that Support Separation of State and Church."

"Thirteen governments [of the original thirteen states] thus founded on the natural authority of the people alone, without a pretence of miracle or mystery, and which are destined to spread over the northern part of that whole quarter of the globe, are a great point gained in favor of the rights of mankind." – Adams, "A Defence of the Constitution of Government of the United States of America" (1787-88), from Adrienne Koch, ed., *The American Enlightenment: The Shaping of the American Experiment and a Free Society* (1965), p. 258, quoted from Ed and Michael Buckner, "Quotations that Support Separation of State and Church."

"We should begin by setting conscience free. When all men of all religions ... shall enjoy equal liberty, property, and an equal chance for honors and power ... we may expect that improvements will be made in the human character and the state of society." – Letter to Dr. Price, April 8, 1785, quoted from Albert Menendez and Ed Doerr, *The Great Quotations on Religious Freedom* (1991).

"As I understand the Christian religion, it was, and is, a revelation. But how has it happened that millions of fables, tales, legends, have been blended with both Jewish and Christian revelation that have made them the most bloody religion that ever existed?" – Letter to F.A. Van der Kamp, December 27, 1816.

Regarding the 1797 Treaty with Tripoli, cited in my letter/article, here is the wording from it regarding the query:

In 1797, six years after the adoption of the Bill of Rights, the United States government signed a treaty with the Muslim nation of Tripoli that contained the following statement (numbered Article 11 in the treaty):

"As *the Government of the United States is not, in any sense, founded on the Christian religion*; as it has in itself no character of enmity against the law, religion or tranquility of Musselmen; and as the states never have entered into any war or act of hostility against any Mohometan nation, it is declared by the parties that no pretext arising from religious opinion shall ever produce an interruption of harmony existing between the two countries."

The treaty was approved by President John Adams and his Secretary of State Timothy Pickering, and was then ratified by the Senate without objection. Of course, today, the U.S., as a secular nation, *should* harbor a natural enmity "against the law, religion and tranquility of Islam," since Islamist jihadists and states that sponsor terrorism have declared war on America, and it *should* bear hostility against any Muslim nation that seeks to harm America.

The historical instances are legion that support the contention that the Founders did not intend America to be a Judeo-Christian state. The Founders may have been deists, but their position was that if God existed, he played no role in human affairs; it was left to men to find the means to achieve happiness on earth through reason, especially in their political arrangements. The Founders were reality oriented; they asserted repeatedly that religious beliefs or fantasies were the purview of individuals, not to be regulated or commanded by the state.

To claim otherwise is to reveal a sorry ignorance of the philosophical and political origins of America; or a patent dishonesty passing for "revealed" truth and masking a frightening political agenda.

The fundamental problem is that our President believes – and I stress *believes* – that America is indeed a nation governed by Christian principles. It is the altruistic, self-sacrificing tenets of the Christian morality that have enmeshed the U.S. in a no-win war in Iraq and Afghanistan against belligerent "Musselmen."

It was clergymen of Bush's ilk who accused Jefferson of wanting to declare war on religion. But it was their "schemes" to impose religion by force that he opposed. It is noteworthy that even in Jefferson's time, while the majority of Americans were nominally Christian, very few of them would likely have disagreed with him (or with Madison or Adams) that the nation was founded on a secular, natural rights philosophy, not a religious one.

Presidential candidates should also take note of it, as well, especially those who in the past evinced no particular religious bent, but who are now jumping on the Gideonite bandwagon. An Associated Press article of July 30th, "Religion Looms Large over 2008 Race," reported:

> "…All the Democratic and Republican presidential hopefuls have been grilled on their religious beliefs. Most seem eager to talk publicly about their faith as they actively court religious voters."

Further into the article, it says:

"The links between religion and governance intensified with the presidency of George W. Bush, said Joan Konner, former dean of the Columbia Journalism School. 'He brought it up when he ran for office and he said his favorite philosopher, in answer to a question in a debate, was Jesus....And then he followed up on that by faith-based public funding and various other actions that started to erode what Americans took for granted as the separation between church and state,' said Konner...."

One of the Associated Press article's examples of a candidate exploiting the religion angle is Democratic Senator Hillary Rodham Clinton, who "emphasizes her Methodist upbringing and says her faith helped her repair her marriage."

So she might claim. It is a more credible likelihood that it was her faith in Bill Clinton's political guidance and savvy and arm-twisting skills that "repaired" her marriage than her belief in the literal truth of the Bible's chapter and verse. Why sacrifice a political career and a chance to satisfy one's power-lust over such a petty thing as a cuckolding spouse? That she is willing to "forgive" her husband's sexual escapades to facilitate her quest for political power is a measure of this ambitious harridan's selflessness and consequent need to "serve society."

However, all the presidential candidates are of the left – name me one Republican who is advocating, for example, repeal of the 16th Amendment, or unregulated laissez faire capitalism, or the absolute right of Americans to be secure in their property – and all of them want to serve "society."

But, as Jamie Whyte writes with sardonic wit in an excellent article in the *Financial Times* of London ("Thatcher was right about society, David," August 2),

"Society is for the left what God is for Christians. Its mere existence creates moral obligations, with no need for contracts and with no need for tiresome debate about the merits of making these obligations law. Those who deny the existence of society are simply trying to evade their responsibilities."

Whyte agrees with former Prime Minister Margaret Thatcher that "there is no such thing as society. There are individual men and women...."

Another way of saying it is that "society" is as much a phantasm as God, and those who believe in it also claim that being a member of it entails duties, responsibilities and debts to it, just as one must obey God's commandments, if one is a conscientious Christian. But if "society" is only the people one encounters in one's lifetime, or sees on television, where is that entity called "society"? And if such a thing does not exist, what is the source of all those duties, obligations and debts? That amorphous mass of strangers sociologists call "society"? As Ayn Rand would put it: *Blank out.*

Both Republicans and Democrats are attempting to wed God and Society in their venal campaigns to win first, the primaries, and then the national election, by appealing to the delusional worst in the electorate: Christian collectivists.

If the left and conservative right combine to create a political force, we may today be witnessing the beginnings of the establishment of a nation the Founders would have abhorred: a theocracy – but with a socialist base.

August 2007

Hearts of Darkness

The moral sewers that are the minds of the likes of Senator Harry Reid of Nevada, and Senate majority leader, were revealed this week with the report that Reid has apologized to President Barack Obama (and to other black civil rights leaders) for having said privately in 2008 that Obama was "light-skinned" and had "no Negro dialect unless he wanted to have one."

Reid's remark was made public in a new book, *Game Change*, by political reporters John Heilemann and Mark Halperin. The book chronicles the sludge and sleaze behind the Democratic contest for presidential nomination and the race against John McCain and Sarah Palin. The publisher's website describes what can only be characterized as a chronicle of dirt:

> *Game Change* answers those questions and more, laying bare the secret history of the 2008 campaign. Heilemann and Halperin take us inside the Obama machine, where staffers referred to the candidate as "Black Jesus." They unearth the quiet conspiracy in the U.S. Senate to prod Obama into the race, driven in part by the fears of senior Democrats that Bill Clinton's personal life might cripple Hillary's presidential prospects....And they reveal how, in an emotional late-night phone call, Obama succeeded in wooing Clinton, despite her staunch resistance, to become his secretary of state.

Reid has apologized for the remark but sounded more like he was campaigning for reelection.

> In a statement, Reid confirmed his remarks and apologized for them. "I deeply regret using such a poor choice of words. I sincerely apologize for offending any and all Americans, especially African Americans for my improper comments," he said today, "I was a proud and enthusiastic supporter of Barack Obama during the campaign and have worked as hard as I can to advance President Obama's legislative agenda. Moreover, throughout my career, from efforts to integrate the Las Vegas strip and the gaming industry to opposing radical judges and promoting diversity in the Senate, I have worked hard to advance issues important to the African American community."

He was forgiven by Obama. Well, of course. Reid, together with Speaker of the House Nancy Pelosi, has the principal task of getting the socialist health-care bill passed by Congress.

> President Barack Obama released a statement this afternoon stating that Reid called him to apologize "for an unfortunate comment." The president said he accepted the apology. "I've seen the passionate leadership he's shown on issues of social justice and I know what's in his heart. As far as I am concerned, the book is closed."

Why would he castigate Reid over a mere slip of tongue and unguarded moment, when more important things are at stake than Obama's own self-respect, such as vanquishing America? But, the book is not closed. *Game Change* goes on sale in a few days, and the guided tour by Heilemann and Halperin of the cesspools of Beltway politics should make the authors millionaires.

This is all very revealing about Harry Reid. It should not be surprising that a man who "advances Obama's legislative agenda" of nationalizing the economy and abridging American freedoms would also harbor the same knee-jerk racist premises as Vice-President Joe Biden and former Senate majority leader Trent Lott. All the minds party to this legislation are vessels of malignity. In public, these creatures appear well-groomed in pressed suits and are on good conduct. Behind the scenes, they are, as Michelle Bachmann of Minnesota suggested, manipulative, foul-mouthed gangsters.

If the Republicans wished to "bring down" Harry Reid as a means of defeating the health-care legislation, they ought to be challenging his political career, premises, and political agenda. They ought to be screaming their heads off about the Marx/Alinsky/Ayers number Reid and his ilk in Congress and the White House are about to pull on the country.

Instead, they are calling for his resignation over a comparatively *unimportant* racial remark. If Reid is guilty of anything, which is his greater offense? Saying something uncouth, or advocating and working hard to bring about the destruction of American liberty?

The Republican ruse to defeat the health-care legislation is intellectually vacuous. The Republican strategy is as ludicrous and futile as if the Romans accused the Huns of being bad dressers, and so they should just go away, instead of pillaging Rome. Harry Reid may be, in the core substance of his existence, a rotten, hypocritical creature. But in the hearts of Republican leadership, there is only the hollow darkness of moral bankruptcy.   *January 2010*

A Mess of Pottage

Having recovered from a despairing disgust with Barack Obama's successful bid for the presidency, I turned my attention to some other matters one could say are cultural partners to that victory deserving of brief attention. While Obama assembles his administration, recruiting some leftover veterans of the Bill Clinton era and some other choice political Pharisees and mountebanks to fill various posts, the news media, which enjoys a larger viewership than newspapers have of readerships, continues to offer through their news desk anchors regurgitated items with patronizing and earnest disingenuousness in cadence with Entertainment Tonight-style segments such as NBC's Matt Lauer in Belize and ABC's Diane Sawyer on the "hot seat."

This is in addition to end-of-broadcast special reports on "making a difference" and "the American spirit," which focus on "giving back," "community service," and other episodes of dutiful selflessness.

All three major news channels, for example, have devoted at least five minutes to where Obama's two daughters will go to school in Washington — a private school, of course, their parents justifiably wary of public schools, into which the president-elect wishes to pour even more billions— and their rooms in the White House. Also, the news media waits breathlessly for the selection of the new White House dog, placing almost as much importance on that as on the composition of Obama's cabinet.

One can take only so much of this kind of pap before developing chronic nausea.

I recently finished reading Albert Jay Nock's *Memoirs of a Superfluous Man* (1943) and will probably also read his *Our Enemy, the State* (1935). Nock was a prolific cultural, political, and social critic in the early 20th century, and has been claimed by libertarians and anarchists of various stripes as one of their intellectual fathers. He is a writer one would like to like. Many of his observations on politics and the arts are so congruent with Ayn Rand's later, similar, but more fundamental observations that one cannot help but suspect that she read his articles in the many periodicals or his many books.

Nock was a pessimist. He came to believe that no matter how perfect a limited government was established, replete with power- and corruption-proof safeguards and checks and balances that would ensure individual liberty and capitalism, it was an incorrigible aspect of human nature for men to find a way to circumvent its architecture, and in the end transform a republican pantheon into a shanty town brothel. There was no point in educating the masses, he wrote, because they would sooner or later take the path of least resistance and favor politicians who promised to convert the marble columns and floor into generous helpings of Brunswick stew for public consumption. He abhorred the "materialism" he witnessed in individuals who sought to secure their material well-being through the pursuit and acquisition of political power over others. He seemed also to have had reservations about individuals who sought that value without wanting to acquire political power.

An ardent admirer of Thomas Jefferson, Nock tempered his admiration of the Founder when discussing the subject of universal public education, which Jefferson advocated. Nock did not believe, as Jefferson did, that education, compulsory or otherwise, necessarily improved one's intelligence or capacity for independent thought.

> "I think…he [Jefferson] would have risked a wry smile at the spectacle of our colleges annually turning out whole battalions of bachelors in the liberal arts who could no more read their diplomas than they could decipher the Minoan linear script. He might also find something to amuse him in the appearance of eminent shysters, jobholders, politicians, and other unscholarly and unsavory characters, on parade in gowns and hoods of the honorary doctorate."

Or addressing graduating classes on the value of selfless service to the community or the nation. However, not once in the *Memoirs* did I encounter a hint that Nock regarded man as a "being of volitional consciousness." He was one himself, but he seems to have overlooked the fact while implicitly denying most other individuals that defining attribute.

Nock rarely involved himself in any political movement of his time, choosing rather to remain a detached observer and commentator, and consequently superfluous.

> "If all I had casually seen…was of the essence of politics, if it was part and parcel of carrying on the country's government, then obviously a decent person could find no place in politics, not even the place of an ordinary voter, for the forces of ignorance, brutality and indecency would outnumber him ten to one."

The recent presidential election would seem to confirm the truth of Nock's assertion; it matters not who would have won this round of politics, Obama or McCain, for each offered a different style of fascism or statism. But that is no excuse to simply resign one's self to the alleged inevitability of decline and destruction. This is what Nock did and it is what he recommended others do, asking his successors to address the "Remnant" and hope for the best.

I concluded that Nock was a kind of fastidious, Epicurean Robert Stadler, the scientific villain in Rand's *Atlas Shrugged* who wailed that since there was no reasoning with people one had to compromise one's principles and accept the status of being rational but irrelevant, and that since most people were ignorant, brutal and indecent, the sole way to deal with them was with force.

Nock did not advocate force to compel men to be rational, but neither was he a consistent exponent of the primacy and efficacy of reason, except among the cultivated and discriminating few (the "Remnant") whom he thought may or may not have any power or chance to instigate cultural change for the better.

One saving grace of Nock was his agreement with Aristotle (and with Rand) that

> "History…represents things only as they are, while fiction represents them as they might and ought to be; and therefore of the two, he adds, 'fiction is the more philosophical and the more highly serious.'"(Nock's own translation from the Greek from Aristotle's *Poetics.*)**

Had he lived long enough (he died in 1945), Nock might have observed the commercial successes of Rand's *The Fountainhead* and *Atlas Shrugged* and their influence in the culture, and perhaps retracted his earlier dismissal of those novels' millions of readers as interchangeable "mass-men," the willing dupes and playthings of criminally-minded politicians.

Speaking of Aristotle's judgment of fiction and history, Stephen Adams in The Daily Telegraph, in a November 6th article, "Novels 'better at explaining world's problems than reports'," discussed that very subject without once mentioning Aristotle. The subject of his article is how fiction can better communicate ideas and the "real life" of people in or from the Third World.

He quotes Dr. Dennis Rodgers of Manchester University's Brooks World Poverty Institute:

"Despite the regular flow of academic studies, expert reports, and policy position papers, it is arguably novelists who do as good a job — if not a better one — of representing and communicating the realities of international development….And fiction often reaches a much larger and diverse audience than academic work and may therefore be more influential in shaping public knowledge and understanding of development issues."

Adams cites three prize-winning novels written by Third World authors, *Brick Lane*, *The Kite Runner*, and *The White Tiger*, as instances of (naturalistic) fiction which, as far as one can determine, not so much have shaped public knowledge and understanding as complemented public policy and sanctioned diversity and multiculturalism.

While some Western academics are lauding fiction as a handmaiden of government social programs, Hollywood continues its bungee free-fall into unreality and fantasy. Bankrupt to the core, except when it has left-wing messages to convey, and unable or unwilling to depict real life heroes and real world conflicts, it has turned more and more to animation, comic books, and graphic novels for material to sustain box office revenues. As evidence of this trend, one website carries an article by Martin Anderson, "75 comics being made into films."

A goodly number of the stories are set in grim futures or in parallel universes, while many others feature magic or heroes with super powers. Only one of them looks promising, *The Megas*, scheduled for release in 2010.

"*Megas* postulates an alternative America where the founding fathers created an aristocracy instead of a democracy, and centers on a detective investigating the seedy underbelly of the American royal family."

The Founders created a rights-protecting republic, not a democracy, as practically everyone today believes they created; the terms, as I have often stressed elsewhere, are *not* synonymous. But the story line is similar to Robert Harris's novel *Fatherland*, in which Nazi Germany won World War Two, and a German police detective in the 1960's investigates the seedy underbelly of the Third Reich to learn that the Holocaust *really* happened. One can only suppose that the story idea's originator was inspired by the fact that many Americans wished to make George Washington a monarch.

All of these films are in some stage of production, but upon their release it is doubtful I will want to see a single one.

It is interesting how fiction — or movies — often apes reality. Many years ago I saw for the first time *The Mouse that Roared* (1959), little realizing at the time that the story line, in which a postage stamp-sized European country declares war on the U.S. for the sole purpose of being defeated and thus qualifying for massive injections of American monetary aid, took its inspiration from history. Is this not what happened in the 1950's, and has happened recently with Mexico, Iraq, Afghanistan, Pakistan, Colombia, and other countries that hate America a little less because of our no-strings-attached aid and financial rescue programs? Peter Sellers in his triple roles in *Mouse* was at least amusing, while his real life counterparts are not.

Art emulated history before history was even made in John Frankenheimer's *The Manchurian Candidate* (1962), a controversial political thriller based on Richard Condon's novel that pre-dated John F. Kennedy's assassination in Dallas the following year. Few films can match its production and esthetic qualities. Its level of intelligence and suspense is impossible to achieve in Hollywood today. (The recent remake of it is utter and politically-correct rubbish.) *The Manchurian Candidate* demands one's full focus to appreciate a single scene or single line of dialogue, much as Howard Hawks' newspaper comedy, *His Girl Friday*, is a perfect, non-stop integration of dialogue and action requiring one's full, undivided attention.

Recently I revisited *The Manchurian Candidate*, and was struck by the performances of James Gregory, as Senator John Yerkes Iselin, and Angela Lansbury, as Mrs. Iselin. Gregory plays an addle-headed, buffoonish politician very reminiscent of President George W. Bush.*** He is putty in the hands of his power-seeking wife, who is too evocative of Hillary Clinton, and who schemes to put her husband in the White House by mostly foul means. She predicts that her husband, at the climax of his party's nomination convention, will rally "a nation of television viewers into a hysteria that will sweep us up into the White House with powers that will make martial law look like anarchy...."

Perhaps we will have a foretaste of that, now that a demagogue will be swept up into the White House to work with a very *simpatico* Congress.

*Memoirs of a Superfluous Man, Hallberg Publishing, 1994 edition, p. 191.

** Ibid, p. 264.
***Note: Today, in January 2012, I would say instead that Vice President Joe Biden is better qualified for that role, as the Obama Administration's "Court Jester."

November 2008

Islam

Reader: Reflect on these statements

Omar Ahmad, the founder of the Council of American-Islamic Relations (CAIR), said to a rally of California Muslims in 1998:

> *"Islam isn't in America to be equal to any other religions, but to become dominant. The Koran, the Muslim book of scripture, should be the highest authority in America, and Islam the only accepted religion unearth."*

And, a quotation by Mohamed Akram, May 19, 1991, from the manifesto of The Muslim Brotherhood:

> *"Eliminating and destroying Western civilization from within and 'sabotaging' its miserable house so that it is eliminated and God's religion is made victorious over all other religions."*

What the Muslim Brotherhood has said about itself since its founding in 1928 by Hasan al-Banna (1906-1949), encapsulated its motto:

> *"God is our goal, the Quran is our Constitution, the Prophet is our leader, jihad is our way, and death in the service of God is the loftiest of our wishes."*

The Muslim Brotherhood has been deemed by the Obama Administration as a "moderate" political force in Egypt. This would be tantamount to deeming Nazism a "moderate" political force. The U.S. is now negotiating with the Taliban over American withdrawal from Afghanistan. This would be tantamount to the FBI negotiating a divvying up of Chicago with Al Capone's gang, with Frank Nitti as the gang's legal counsel.

Enough said? Clear enough. Plain as day? If not, then here it is from the horse's mouth. Or Mohammad's. This is from a page from Bridgette Gabriel's *Act for America* blog site. This is a sampling of *Suras* from the *Koran*:

61:19 "...*that He (Muhammad) may make it* **conqueror of all religion** *however much idolaters may be averse*" + **48:28** "...*to proclaim it over all religion*" + **9:33** "...*prevail over all religions*" **8:39** *and* **2:193** "...*and religion should be* **only for Allah**" +**3:189** "*And Allah's is the kingdom of the heavens and the earth...*"

January 2012

The Fakirs of Reality

Raymond Ibrahim, an associate director of The Middle East Forum, wrote an article for Pajamas Media, "The Ultimate Lesson of Egypt's Faked Photo." In it he explains why a leading Mideast newspaper, *Al Ahram*, decided to run a doctored photograph of Egyptian president Hosni Mubarak.

> One of the most widely circulated newspapers in the world, Egypt's *Al Ahram*, recently ran a fake picture depicting Egyptian President Hosni Mubarak walking in front of U.S. President Barack Obama and a pack of other Mideast leaders [at the White House]. In fact, based on the original photo, Mubarak, the octogenarian, appeared trailing last.

So poor in pride and apparently also in intellectual honesty, and desperate for recognition of some important role that Egypt was playing in world affairs, the editor rationalized the deception:

> *Al Ahram* editor Ossama al-Saraya defended the fraudulent photo by referring to it as an "expressionist photo ... a brief, live and true expression of the prominent stance of President Mubarak in the Palestinian issue, his unique role in leading it before Washington." All well and good, but beyond the euphemisms and rationalizations, the fact remains: by portraying something that was not true, the state-run *Al Ahram* intentionally tried to deceive the people.

الإنترنت رائع وه عظيم! *The Internet is great!* Some Egyptians, however, don't appreciate the effort, reports Ibrahim.

> As Wael Khalil, the Egyptian blogger who first called attention to the altered photo, pointed out, this anecdote is a snapshot of the routine deception the Egyptian government foists on the people: "They lie to us all the time. Instead of addressing the real issues, they just Photoshop it."

Very reminiscent of how President Barack Obama and his administration report the successful "reality" of their programs and policies in their repeated and unsuccessful attempts to deceive the American people. But, that is another story. It is also reminiscent of the "toilet paper" fatwa pronounced on a German blogger who reported

Edward Cline

that Fatwa No. 40378 in the *Encyclopedia of Fatwas* specified that the New Testament and Torah could be used as toilet paper. Ever defiant, she also featured a graphic of the Koran as a roll of not-so-Charmin. That exercise in freedom of speech earned her a death fatwa. Nevertheless, Fatwa No. 40378 was removed from the *Encyclopedia* site in an attempt to deceive. Read the story here.

However, I am reminded by Ibrahim's article of an episode of "Seinfeld," in which George, the neurotic moocher, liar, schemer, and ne'er-do-well, buys a car from a used car salesman who tells him, quite tongue-in-cheek, that it was once owned by Jon Voight, the actor. George buys the car for that sole reason, and his chronically tenuous self-esteem is inflated because now he can boast to distraction that he owns a car once owned and driven by a famous person. It turns out that the car was indeed owned by a "John Voight," by a near-namesake but not by the actor. George's new-found self-esteem rapidly deflates like a defective balloon.

The episode described by Ibrahim here of the newspaper faking a photograph of Hosni Mubarak's falsified place in the scheme of things is equally pathetic, and also points to a problem not only with Islam but with Muslim "culture." If by a "culture" we mean a set of fundamental beliefs and practices shared by a specific group of people, then Muslim "culture" is fraught with many deterministic and nihilistic premises grounded on one core tenet which Islam shares with Christianity and any other religion: the assertion of an unprovable existence of a supreme being, one who authored creation and who is either omniscient or omnipotent, or, paradoxically, both.

The name of this being is immaterial. The formation of a moral code based on the belief in the existence and power of a ghost that no one has ever seen (except, apocryphally, by Moses in the Old Testament) is destined, and arguably even intended, to inculcate and encourage a dishonesty (in this case, Koran-sanctioned *taqiya*) that manifests itself in countless forms even among those who are not particularly avid devotees to the religion, including indifferent Muslims-in-name-only ("moderates") and alleged secularists such as Hosni Mubarak and the newspaper's editor. The tenet requires men to work against the evidence of their senses, and often to pretend that some things are "real" and significant, even though no one can observe them. It requires them to fake reality, to appeal to an attribute of man that the creed denigrates (faith is "superior" to reason) in order to perpetrate or perpetuate a lie, a fraud, or a myth.

While dwelling on how Islam and Muslim culture are mutually crippling in terms how the creed especially corrupts a society that is not entirely founded on an esteem for truth, Ibrahim notes:

41

...if Muslim culture is more tenacious and consequential than Muslim doctrine, still, the former has strong roots in the latter. Thus, while radical Muslims *consciously* seek to uphold the letter of the law, moderates *unconsciously* adhere to its cultural, social, and political manifestations.

Lest one still doubt that aspects of a religion can become casually embedded in the social fabric of a civilization, one need look no further than to Christianity, which continues to exhibit a strong, albeit unconscious, influence on the secular West, including upon those who most disavow it. After all, tolerance, human rights, a desire for peace, being the "nice guy"— indeed, all of those concepts most championed by today's liberal secularist, did not develop out of a vacuum, but rather out of a 2,000-year-old Christian heritage that preached what was then absurd and today aberrant, but which nonetheless jibes so well with the West's secular mindset. Surely not a coincidence.

The phenomena of dishonesty and willingness to fake reality may be observed in cultures dominated by Christianity, as well. Witness the recent statements by Pope Benedict XVI in Britain that atheism or "godlessness" can only lead to Nazism, when in fact Nazism was founded on its own virulent brand of mysticism, with Hitler as its "prophet" (and it was mostly German Protestants who buttressed his regime, with a major assist by the knowledge-repressing Vatican) espousing the superiority of the German race and culture, Germany's "rightful" place in the scheme of things, its "destiny" to rule the globe (an Islamic dream, as well), the elevation of instinct and force over reason, and so on.

In his address, the Pope spoke of "a Nazi tyranny that wished to eradicate God from society." He went on to urge the UK to guard against "aggressive forms of secularism.

He said: "Even in our own lifetimes we can recall how Britain and her leaders stood against a Nazi tyranny that wished to eradicate God from society and denied our common humanity to many, especially the Jews, who were thought unfit to live. As we reflect on the sobering lessons of atheist extremism of the 20th century, let us never forget how the exclusion of God, religion and virtue from public life leads ultimately to a truncated vision of man and of society and thus a reductive vision of a person and his destiny."

Churchill and Roosevelt did not fight Nazi tyranny solely because it sought to "eradicate God from society." They fought it because it was tyranny. Benedict knows this. But, there he was, faking reality, begging the faithful not to abandon God by listening to those advocates of "atheist extremism," because that would only lead to a repetition of the horrors of the 20th century.

But, there is an old, non-atheistic nemesis rising unopposed, and that is Islam. Historically, Christianity has acted like a ball-and-chain on Western civilization, hampering its progress and muting its capacity to foster human happiness. Nevertheless, men were and still are able to move forward. Islam promises destroy Western civilization from within and without, to condemn men to a state of miserable and permanent stagnation, and is the author of horrors past, present, and for the foreseeable future.

I disagree with Ibrahim's random list of benign concepts that were "casually embedded" by a ubiquitous Christian morality in Western civilization — he omits individual rights, which are not the same as the vague notion of unspecified "human rights," which any statist or power-seeker can champion by just filling in the blanks, while "tolerance" can also mean a toleration, and, by extension, a sanction of the irrational — but he is right that "the teachings of a religion can subtly color the worldview of its non-observant posterity." Not only subtly, but dramatically, such as America's self-sacrificing effort to "remake" Iraq and Afghanistan into so-called 'democracies."

The ultimate solution for "moderate" Muslims who wish to reform Islam and chuck its poisonous and tribalist influence in Muslim "culture" (whatever that may be, aside from the equally faked "Golden Age" of Islam and Cordoba) is to abandon Islam altogether and discover and advocate reason in all things, especially in all things moral. They must acknowledge, in such a commitment, that there is no room in reason for Allah, God, or faith. They must grasp that Islam cannot be "reformed" without turning it into a "ghost" of its former self.

They, as Ayaan Hirsi Ali and other notable "apostates" have done, must recognize that Islam, like Christianity, is a used car lot clunker or a money pit and was never a great deal even when it was new. It was once owned by scimitar-wielding thug who falsely claimed it won a NASCAR race, but it will require fortunes in labor and parts to keep it in running order as a "living" religion. "Moderate" Muslims should just cut their losses and walk away from it, and discover a philosophy of reason.

Reality cannot be Photoshopped. And the man who begs that it be, is a fakir who deserves the scorn of all who value the truth.

September 2010

Our Islamic Nemesis, Then and Now

Browsing through the thousands of pages of a diplomatic history of the United States commissioned by the State Department, I came across this interesting paragraph about the efforts and obstacles of the U.S. to establish civil relations with foreign powers under the Articles of Confederation, before adoption of the Constitution:

> "The Confederation's lack of power was an even more significant factor in the abortive negotiations over American sailors held captive in Algiers. Unlike relations with Spain...Algiers held all the advantages. The guarantee of safe passage in the Mediterranean was always available: namely, to pay suitable tribute to the Dey [Muhammad III, Emperor of Morocco, 1757-1790]. This route was followed by European powers, who found it less expensive to pay the pirates than to fight them. Such recourse was not open to Americans. Although the issue was never as vital to America's survival as other problems in foreign relations, none was more painful. For Jefferson, who was given the task of ransoming the American captives, the solution lay in arms. He wanted to join a federation that would sweep the pirates from the sea once and for all, and was distressed over France's submitting to Algerine demands. [John] Jay's reaction was more cynical; he sensed that Europe had no interest in challenging the pirates, and would relish the prospect of a war between America and the Barbary States, from which Europe would benefit...."*

Jefferson at this time was minister to France, and John Jay minister to Spain. What impressed me was the echo from that distant era of Europe's toleration of the Barbary pirates, in particular France's, and Europe's unwillingness to "sweep the pirates from the sea once and for all." The U.S., at the time strapped for cash to launch a navy that would have satisfied Jefferson's recommendation, could do little else but emulate the European policy and pay tribute. In 1786 the U.S. representative, John Barclay, negotiated a "non-molestation" treaty with Morocco, whose "emperor" was paid $10,000 in gifts to sign it. But Tripoli, Algiers and Tunis for the next three decades continued their seizures of American vessels and enslaving their crews and passengers. After the Dey's death, Morocco also resumed its depredations.

It should be noted here that during the American Revolution and the Napoleonic Wars, Barbary pirates would turn over seized American vessels to the British navy! For a price, of course.

As president, Jefferson took the first concrete steps to counter the Barbary looters by sending a squadron to combat Tripoli, which had declared war on the U.S. because it didn't think it was receiving enough in tribute. (For details, see the adventures of Stephen Decatur). Jefferson, struggling with a contentious Congress, was unable to deal effectively with the other Barbary States. It fell to President James Madison to finish the task of reducing Algiers, Tunis, Morocco and Tripoli and forcing them to cease their plundering of American vessels (1815).

One must observe that neither Jefferson, Jay or Madison responded to the Barbary "crisis" by proposing to "democratize" the Barbary States for the sake of "peace" in the Mediterranean, or rebuild towns damaged by American bombardments, or pay compensation to "innocent" Muslims affected by the fighting. And all they got in the way of European response to the idea of an international military effort to subdue the Barbary States was indifference and expressions of "such is life" tolerance of Barbary extortion. Further, Jay was correct in his assessment of Europe, in that it benefited from American action at no cost to it, not even in an expression of gratitude. Today, Europe is similarly benefiting at the expense of the U.S. expending blood and treasure fighting the wrong war.

The historical parallels of and differences between that age and this one are noteworthy, not only in terms of actions taken, but in terms of a nation asserting its right to reply to force with force. Jefferson and Madison were not by nature "men of war," but they nonetheless settled on war instead of continuing to pay tribute to barbarians and submitting to their extortion. Their decisions were not governed by an unreasoning, emotional anathema to "violence." In that era, the U.S. had to wait until it was solvent enough to dispatch a navy to end the "crisis." And when the causes of the "crisis" were dealt with, there was no more crisis to bedevil the country.

When one watches the frantic, contemptible relief with which the U.S. and Europe react to the least chance for "peace" between Israel and Lebanon (re the recent U.N. Security Council resolution to end the fighting, but condescending to allow Israel to defend itself), one cannot help but sense that it is not "peace" they are seeking, but release from the responsibility of taking a moral stand, in this instance, on the right of Israel to retaliate with force against a power seeking its destruction. Thus, Hezbollah, a more vicious and dangerous band of killers than the Barbary pirates ever could be (they were not being financed with

Iranian oil revenues), is being treated as an ineluctable metaphysical fact that must be dealt with on its own terms.

The absence of a moral stand treats the warring parties, Israel and Hezbollah (or Lebanon, if you like, which one observer called a "state within a terrorist organization"), to morally neutral entities fighting doing violence to each other for no comprehensible reason.

Somehow, think President Bush, Condoleezza Rice, Prime Minister Blair, France and other parties, the perilous conflict in the Mideast can be reduced to the level of a Hatfield-McCoy feud of "proportionate," tit-for-tat "reciprocal" actions, refereed by the United Nations, which has in the past, more than once, demonstrated a virulent hatred of Israel (and of the U.S.).

Underscoring the nature of the conflict, King Abdullah of Jordan, who has criticized the U.S. and Israel over the war, according to the BBC, "stressed the only way to achieve peace was to end the Israeli occupation of Arab lands."

Concretely, he was referring to the territories Israel won and kept after being attacked by its Arab neighbors. More broadly, he was referring to the claim by Hezbollah, by the Palestinians, by Syria, by Iran, that Israel itself "occupies' Arab land, and that its destruction would bring "peace" to the Mideast.

A moral stand in this and in any other "crisis" that involves aggression would be a refusal to sacrifice the good to evil and a "proactive" policy to preserve the good. This is not our present policy. Now we are asking Israel, the good, what one commentator called the "frontline of civilization in the Mideast," to jeopardize its existence by accommodating an unacknowledged evil, Islamofascism. This is a totalitarian movement which, as one Iranian ayatollah recently proclaimed, will one day rule from Spain to Iran, by jihad or by diplomacy.

There would be no need for a U.N. sponsored "international" force to patrol the Israeli-Lebanese border if Israel were allowed to eradicate Hezbollah "once and for all." As for the Lebanese government, it should fall. The Lebanese should learn the hard way that it should not pay to form a "democratic" alliance with totalitarian killers.

Our Islamic enemies understand us, all too well, and are advancing because they grasp that the West is unwilling to assert not only its right to exist, but its moral superiority. When will our political leaders begin to understand our enemies and act to vanquish them? Only when they grasp the fact that retaliatory violence is the only answer to force and terror.

*From *The Emerging Nation: Foreign Relations of the United States Under the Articles of Confederation, 1780-89*, Vol. 3. National Historical Publications and Records Commission, 1996

August 2006

The Muslims' New Program for Thought Control

"As we trace the genius of a nation by their taste in poetry and music, so by their encouragement of these we may judge of their rise or fall; good authors have never been wanting in happy climes. Barbarism begins her reign by banishing the Muses. Those who have ears to hear, let them hear!"

So wrote Philip Dormer Stanhope, the Earl of Chesterfield, in 1749 in a preface to a pamphlet of his speech in the House of Lords against the proposed *Act for Licensing the Stage*, an act supported by politicians who were being mocked in theaters by satire to the applause of an appreciative public.

In a not so coincidental dovetailing of events, a bill to regulate "hate speech" is at present being debated in the British parliament that would make it a criminal offense to publicly disparage any creed or set of religious beliefs, in addition to "inciting" violence via words or pictures against members of any race or religious sect. Ostensively, the bill is aimed at Muslims who call for jihad in Britain; in effect, it will silence anyone who questions or criticizes any creed or system of beliefs. The bill aims to suppress the provocation of thugs and rioters by gagging those who would call them thugs and rioters.

It will silence everyone but the Muslims.

At the same time, the Muslim "furor" over the publication and republication in Danish and European newspapers of cartoons that caricature Mohammed, whose depiction in any form is regarded as blasphemy, shocked many Westerners from their multicultural apathy. The one cartoon that seems to have touched the Muslim nerve — shall we call it "sensitivity"? — shows the head of Mohammed wearing a turban shaped as a lit-fuse bomb. This was a caricature that summed up the thousands of murders and scale of destruction wrought by Islamic "martyrs" and jihadists over the past thirty years. It was an astute, stylistic observation, a justifiable estimate of the means and ends of Islamic fascism.

The pit felt at the bottom of many stomachs over this new demand of the Muslims is fear: fear of mindless retribution, of death and destruction. It causes those who feel it to shut up in the name of "respect" for Muslim beliefs. This is the true nature of the "respect" of major American news organizations, such as CBS, when it refused to show a single cartoon.

The pit felt at the bottom of other stomachs is resolve, of a determination to stand up now for the freedom to say what one thinks, with the knowledge that if the West capitulates to Muslim demands, it will have surrendered the key freedom that permits the fight for all the other freedoms. Many European newspapers have defied Muslim "sensibilities" and reprinted the cartoons.

Islamic spokesmen called this action a "provocation." But what is it that is being "provoked"? Violence. Property destruction. Kidnappings. Murders. The initiation of physical force and terror. All in the name of Mohammed and Allah. Hardly the behavior of a "pacific" religion that would persuade one that it just wants to "get along."

Implied in the claim that images of Mohammed constitute blasphemy, is that anyone who creates such an image is guilty of blasphemy. What the Muslims are demanding is that non-Muslims accept that religious tenet. Thus, "respect" by non-Muslims of the tenet, at the price of surrendering the right to criticize Islam, means virtual conversion to Islam, a major step in the direction of actual conversion.

Islamists see the implications of multiculturalism and "diversity" much better than do the advocates and practitioners of these secular "creeds." Islamists are infamous for not subscribing to multiculturalism and diversity. They might claim that it is not conversion they seek, but "respect." But if one does not "respect" a belief, it is one's right to question it, or to criticize it in a book, essay, speech, or cartoon.

However, if one "respects" it, then it becomes a taboo subject, off limits to reasoned enquiry and civil discussion. One tells oneself: I have no right to say anything about it. And if one is prohibited, under penalty of prosecution, intimidation, or physical violence, from saying or writing anything about it, then there is no reason or point to thinking of it, either.

What a formula for thought control!

The Islamists know it. Most Western intellectuals and politicians do not.

It is time that Muslims here and abroad got used to "offensive" portrayals of Mohammed, and, for good measure, of Allah himself. After all, no one is forcing them to look at the cartoons. The West regularly shrugs off the pictorial vilification of Western institutions, culture, creeds, persons and icons. Anyone familiar with the Arab press and Arab websites will note how vicious Muslim cartoonists are.

That would be a fair trade, would it not, an exercise in mutual "tolerance" and good will? One might say that the solution to the problem is reciprocity. The Arab press can publish vicious cartoons of the West, and the West can publish mildly "offensive" cartoons about Islam.

But it is not an issue of reciprocity. Reciprocity is not in the Islamic agenda. "Islam" means "submission," and it is submission its ill-willed mullahs and imams demand in exchange for the "peace" of intellectual torpidity in their rank and file followers, as well as in the West. Islam is by its very nature intolerant of other creeds and requires absolute, mindless obedience of Allah and compliance with the prophet's commandments. It cannot be "reformed" as Christianity has been. Even the new Pope, Benedict XVI, has conceded that. There are no concessions Islam could possibly make without triggering its self-destruction. Fundamentally, there is no such thing as a "moderate" Muslim or a "civilized" Islam, not when the core beliefs of the *Koran* and commands of the *Hadith* sanction the murder and enslavement of non-Muslims in an on-going jihad that will end only with the establishment of a global caliphate.

Islamic spokesman claim that they do not seek to crush freedom of speech or expression, only to put "limits" on it. Ultimately, however, any "limit" on speech means no expression, no freedom to say what one thinks must be said. It means not reaching a conclusion, and settling for only half a syllogism, or none at all. It means that an idea has been removed from debate, discussion, and criticism.

This is a defining moment for the West. It must either speak up in defense, and in bold, unapologetic assertion, of the idea of freedom of speech, or forever cringe in "respect" of Islamic tenets, much as in the film *The Godfather*, the favor-seeking mortician cringed when gangster Vito Corleone accused him of not granting him "respect." The fearful mortician immediately offered his respect and submission. He was seeking mere vengeance; Corleone required submission and acknowledgement of his power.

This will logically require the ultimate scrapping of another "belief" system, that of multiculturalism and diversity, and their recognition as fatal fallacies.

Ever since the Renaissance the genius of the West has been a commitment to the freedom of men to question the moral claims of others. Reason has always settled the question. Islamists are demanding that the West banish the Muse of Reason. Let those who have ears, hear that demand and understand its fundamental requirement. And let those who understand it, speak now, or forever maintain a "respectful" silence.

February 2006

Is "Islamophobia" *Justified?*

I would not blanch if I were ever charged with "Islamophobia." "Islam" means "submission," or subjugation to religious tyranny. The root Greek term phobia means fear. The American Heritage Dictionary and other American dictionaries cite two meanings of phobia: the first is a persistent, abnormal, or illogical fear of a specific thing; the second is a strong fear, dislike, or aversion. The Oxford English Dictionary defines phobia as "fear, horror, or aversion, especially of a morbid character."

I confess that, yes, I have a morbid fear of Islam, for I know its means and ends, which are incompatible with my existence as a free, thinking man.

Yes, I harbor a strong dislike of Islam, and of anyone who defends it, or submits to it, or dismisses it as nothing to worry about (Islamists, say their Western apologists, really don't mean to conquer anyone, they just want to "get along").

And, yes, I have a resolute aversion for Islam, because of what it requires of men, which is the abdication of their minds and selves, their abandonment of reason as a guide to the conduct of their lives, together with the substitution of a ghost's and others' dictates as their "moral" guide, and their consequent and necessary membership in the ranks of an enemy army.

In this context, "Islamophobia" can be defined as a fear of being under the rule of a theocracy — any theocracy — but especially a tyranny that promises death, dismemberment, or slavery for anyone not submitting to it. Any doubt about its means and ends ought to be dispelled by citing just one of the many verses from the Koran that prescribe the fate of non-believers in Allah to develop a healthy fear of Islam: "They (infidels) will be killed or crucified, or have their hands and feet on alternate sides cut off."

So, call me an infidel. As a novelist and writer, I take words at their literal meanings. That verse is not a euphemistic proverb that could by any means be interpreted as an expression of a Muslim's personal "inner struggle" for faith or an overture of peaceful coexistence, as Islamic scholars would have us believe. What commentators frequently overlook is the fact that these same scholars do not contest the English translation of those verses. Ambiguity in language ought to trigger anyone's suspicions. Never mind those scholars' reassurances that it doesn't mean what it says; feet are feet and hands are hands. Clarity such as can be found in the Koran about the many unambiguous ways that infidels, Jews, and other "people of

52

the book" should be treated ought to provoke revulsion and opposition. Or even a phobia.

The inspiration of this observation was a transcript of a debate televised on Al-Jazeera on July 26th, 2005 between Wafa Sultan, a psychiatrist and former Muslim living in hiding in Los Angeles, and Dr. Ahmad Bin Muhammad, an Algerian professor of religious politics and an Islamist. Sultan was just as acerbic in her condemnation of Islam as Oriana Fallaci, the outspoken Italian journalist, while Bin Muhammad was not only vitriolic but blind-sided by her articulate, courageous and uncompromising apostasy. President Bush ought to be required to spend a day with her at Camp David, and less time consulting with glad-handing conciliators Condi Rice and Karen Hughes. Perhaps he would emerge from that encounter shaken but with a more efficacious policy of dealing with this country's enemies.

A phobia, of course, is usually an irrational or unreasoning mental condition. Its object is typically spiders, snakes, mice, heights or some other mundane phenomena. But, it can be fixed on a very real nemesis and have a rational basis. In this instance, the nemesis is an ideology closed to reason, one that could destroy the countless values that constitute Western civilization and make life a living hell (provided one is not first killed or crucified) if one remembered what was lost, or at best a miasmatic existence of servitude to the anointed and privileged, of joyless drudgery and degrading ritual.

A thinking person will move from his phobia to an analysis of what it is he fears and a method for combating it. One graduates from that to a healthy contempt for Islam and all things mystical. One should become almost coldly dispassionate about it, allowing one to formulate arguments against it and for its antidote.

Still, if I am ever accused of being an "Islamophobe," I will reply with two thumbs up and my most charming smile.

Islam is not the only nemesis threatening civilization. Free men are faced today with a steady diminution of their freedom at the hands of their own political leadership, whether the anti-American Left, the religious, God-fearing Right, or a "moderate" mix of the two, as the scope of especially federal power exercised in all realms of life continues to expand and suffocate liberty. Free men are besieged on two fronts: at home, where the enemies of freedom wish to regulate it out of existence in the name of the "public good"; and from abroad, in the name of Allah. If one wants to understand why our political leadership will not or is unable to oppose Islamofascism, consider the mutuality of ends of both parties: the incremental erasure of freedom with subtle and not-so-subtle applications of force.

Homage and unthinking loyalty to multiculturalism, "tolerance," and political correctness save our political leadership and most of our intellectuals the soul-searching bother of examining the consequences of either their own actions and policies or those of this country's enemies. They are literally daft about "democracy," believing it gives them leave to turn productive Americans into a tax revenue generating dhimmi (or subjugated population, a term invented by historian Bat Ye'or as a consequence of her study of populations conquered by Islam).

The Democrats and Republicans are still beholden to Roosevelt's Brunswick stew of the "four freedoms," which have served as the unchallenged coda of our burgeoning welfare state, soaring national debt, and foreign policy. While the mentally myopic rant about the most irrelevant matters ("I have a right not to get breast cancer from second-hand smoke," "I have a right to wheelchair access to anywhere I want to go," "I have a right to sue a company for my stupid use of its product," "I have a right to affordable medical care," and so on), and legislators promise to do something about them, a predator lurks beyond our shores, loping impatiently in the darkening forests of Eurabia for a chance to strike us again. It settles for the time being for the gang rape of a Swedish woman or the murder of a Dutch filmmaker or the torture and murder of a French Jew. But its glance always returns to America, where its proxies, such as CAIR, are busy preparing the ground for conquest here, as well. Islam's appetite is boundless.

Belgium's population is approaching the fifty percent Muslim mark, and that country may be the first in Europe to succumb politically to Islamist conquest. This would be ironic justice, considering the bureaucratic dictatorship headquartered in Brussels that goes by the name of the European Union. Perhaps the name of this nascent regime will be revised to the "Eurabian Union." Doubtless those "freely elected" mullahs and imams will insist on it. But one can bet that when it happens, all of Europe's tolerant multiculturalists will be the first to feel the ax blades on their necks or the stilettos in their hearts, if they don't first emigrate to safer shores. Just one look at the state of Europe would be enough to give any sane man a phobia, and vow to never let it happen here.

But it *is* happening here under the politics of "progressive democracy," or incremental socialism and the "socialization" of a public school educated, dumbed down citizenry. Progressivism has been the stealthy nullification or expropriation of property rights and, most recently, the abridgement of freedom of speech. A citizenry "conditioned" to tolerate the legalized banditry of our government will tolerate or remain insensate to the seductive but deceptive blandishments of Islamism.

Consider the cluelessness of the colleagues of an American "peace worker" taken hostage months ago and recently found dead near a Baghdad rubbish heap, his body riddled with bullets and obviously tortured before being executed. What was their response to the news? Not outrage, or anger, or even a word of vengeance. Just humility and an incomprehension that can be traced to the scuttling of their rationality by altruism. "He was working for peace, why would anyone want to kill him?" Despite the tank car trains of Western blood spilled by Islamist killers over the past thirty years, altruism prevents them from grasping that the killers are not interested in peace and do not grant good-intentioned, unarmed peace workers any kind of immunity or dispensation. The beasts are jihadists, and American journalists, peace workers and soldiers are their interchangeable targets. "Good intentions" to jihadists are an invitation to conquest.

Speaking of good intentions, there is President Bush with his willingness to sacrifice American lives and wealth in a Wilsonian policy to "democratize" the Mideast, instead of defending this country. The phenomena of the clueless peace workers and Bush's suicidal foreign policy are intimately linked by altruism.

And too often now, when I consider my fellow Americans and the death grip that altruism has on their minds and actions, I feel a phobia coming on.

March 2006

"Islamophobia" *is Justified*

Islam gets such good Western press that one can't imagine why Muslims protest so much. For every "offensive" cartoon of Mohammad that bubbles up into public view from the fetid swamp of a decaying and suicidal European culture, there are miles of newsprint that implicitly or overtly take the side of Islam. Of course, the "public" is fortunate if it ever sees these cartoons, because most Western newspapers and news services are too tremulously funked to reprint them for their readers' edification. The cowardice is artfully disguised by most publications under the cloak of multicultural "tolerance" and "respect" for a great religion.

The exceptions are perhaps such bastions of freedom of the press as The *New York Times*, which, so much the worse, seems to be sincere in its esteem for a creed whose chaotic and often homicidal tenets were established by a murderous barbarian who heard a voice in the night. The angel Gabriel's, the legend goes. One imagines Allah was too much of elitist snot to speak directly to a mere mortal.

The Islamists' or Islamofascists' protests against such alleged "offenses" seem all out of proportion to their infrequent occurrences. This is because the Islamists demand complete, across-the-board "respect" – or *submission*. Islam forbids Muslims to criticize the creed; its fundamentalists also expect infidels to abide by the same prohibition.

An instance of Islam-friendly journalism is an Associated Press item of September 16, under the headline "U.N. expert: Religious bias a threat to peace." No, the "religious bias" is not Islam's persecution and murder of Christians, Jews, and other religious faithful around the world, but a phenomenon called "Islamophobia."

> "A U.N. expert on racism on Friday branded the defamation of religions – in particular critical portrayals of Islam in the West – a threat to world peace.

> "Islamophobia today is the most serious form of religious defamation,' Doudou Diene told the U.N. Human Rights Council, which is holding a three-week session in Geneva.

> "Diene cited a caricature of the Muslim Prophet Muhammad in a Swedish newspaper, a protest by far-right groups in Belgium Tuesday against the 'Islamization of Europe,' and campaigns

against the construction of mosques in Germany and of an 'ever increasing trend' toward anti-Islamic actions in Europe."

One's first thought after reading this pap is: "He must be kidding." But, then, Mr. Diene is a U.N. "expert," and such "experts" not only get things backwards, but get them perversely backwards, as well. No one notices it, perhaps least of all Western journalists.

> "Diene, a Senegalese lawyer and U.N. expert on racism, was presenting a report on defamation of religions to the 47-member council. The report also includes sections on anti-Semitism and other forms of persecution around the world."

If Mr. Diene asserted in his report that "Islamophobia" is the "most serious form of religious defamation," then one can bet that the sections on anti-Semitism and "other forms of persecution" will not be very lengthy or sententious. If they exist, these sections will not dwell on:

> ➤ The regular defamation in cartoons, editorials and in television programming of Jews, Christians and other religionists in the Muslim media.
> ➤ The Islamic Sudanese government's campaign of genocide and ethnic cleansing in Darfur.
> ➤ The fatwas against the Danish and Swedish cartoonists (not to mention the still outstanding fatwa against Salman Rushdie, and the achieved fatwas against Pim Fortuyn and Theo van Gogh).
> ➤ The destruction or vandalizing of churches and attacks on non-Muslims during Muslim riots in Europe, especially against non-hijabed, non-Muslim women.
> ➤ The synagogues in many European cities now protected by the police or private armed guards against Muslim jihadists.

That is just the tip of the iceberg.

The Associated Press item concludes:

> "African and Islamic countries welcomed the assessment and called for moves to draft an international treaty that would compel states to act against any form of defamation of religion.

European Union members of the council and other countries cautioned against equating criticism of religion with racism."

The only religionists now claiming that any criticism of Islam by Westerners constitutes "racism" are Muslims. And the "caution" by Europeans and presumably other Western nations on the council is the usual meekly vacuous squeak of protest.

None of this was noted by Frank Jordans, who filed the AP report. Now, before he filed his article, he might have taken time to consult a dictionary on the term "phobia." The *Concise Oxford English Dictionary* defines it as a "morbid fear or aversion." *Webster's New Collegiate* defines it as "an irrational, persistent fear of a particular object or class of objects." The *American Heritage* defines it as "a persistent, abnormal, or illogical fear of a specific thing or situation."

He might have then asked himself: If Islamists or jihadists in the name of Allah were not so regularly persistent in their suicide bombings, detected and foiled conspiracies to perpetrate mass casualties in the West, kidnappings and murders of non-Muslim humanitarian workers, and other episodes of Islamic religious violence, would anyone be justified in developing a "phobia" for Islam? No.

However, since all these outrages are committed by Muslims in the name of Islam, could "Islamophobia" be considered at all morbid, irrational, illogical or even abnormal? Is such a phobia any less justified or understandable than harboring a phobia for rattlesnakes, black widow spiders, or poisonous centipedes?

Perhaps, he might have further thought, such a phobia is more justified or understandable because, while one might have a chance but fatal encounter with a snake, spider or centipede, Islamists or Islamofascists deliberately target their victims. The difference, he might have realized, is one of volition.

Then the journalist might have scoffed: Who or what is the real "threat to world peace"? How can this U.N. "expert" take so much exception to the defiant but pathetic gestures of a dying culture – the cartoons, the protest against the Islamization of Europe and so on – and characterize them as "destabilizing"?

And, if he had any self-respect as a journalist, and respect for his profession, he might have taken principled exception to the idea of an "international treaty" that would prohibit or punish the defamation of any religion. He might have thought: I'll say what I damned well please about any religion. As far as I'm concerned, and based on all the evidence of the last thirty years of Islamic violence, Islam has earned that phobia.

Jordans could have enlightened his readers about the Swedish cartoon mentioned by Doudou Diene – of Mohammad's head on the body of a dog, a mullah holding the dog leash – drawn by Lars Vilks and published in *Nerikes Allehanda* on August 18. He could have mentioned the $100,000 reward for the murder of Vilks and a $50,000 reward for murdering the newspaper's editor, both offered by the purported head of Al Quada in Iraq, Abu Omar al-Baghdadi.

Whose "peace" was threatened? Islam's, or the Swedes'? These questions did not occur to Jordans, and so he did not bother to enlighten his readers.

Jordans could have enlightened his readers about the "far-right protests in Belgium against the 'Islamization of Europe.'" These protests occurred in Brussels on September 11, when a peaceful protest by members of Belgium's opposition parties was broken up by Belgian police, who beat and arrested two prominent demonstrators. The police undoubtedly wanted to prove to Islamists that they are on their side and can be just as brutal when it comes to punishing anyone who publicly speaks on the danger of recognizing Sharia law in an expiring Western culture.

Jordans could have questioned the use of the term "far-right" when it is used to smear anyone who protests Islamization anywhere, and emphasized that while it has traditionally been the "far right" that is accused of using "police state" tactics to squelch opposition, any more it is the far left that is employing them, such as in Belgium.

Jordans' investigative skills must have been in a sleep mode on this subject, too.

Finally, Jordans could have mentioned another instance of anti-Islamic action in Europe cited by Diene, the "campaigns against the construction of mosques in Germany and Switzerland." He might have merely noted these campaigns, and posed the question of whether they alone can stem the tide of Islamization, then proposed that it is the totalitarian ideas that are the foundation of Islam which must be combated, not their manifestation in the form of mosques. (He might have even pointed out that no synagogues, churches or even chapels may be built in Saudi Arabia and other Islamic fiefdoms, and delved into the Islamists' double standard on the matter of places of worship.)

Jordans could have written something like this:

> "In the West, churches and synagogues are just that – places for people to go and worship and socialize. But in the West, as well as in the Middle East, and in Indonesia and other Muslim-dominated countries, most mosques are venues of rabble-

rousing and jihadist recruiting, where imams and mullahs regularly declaim against the West for its sins against Allah and call for holy war. This has been so thoroughly documented by intelligence services that it is a wonder most mosques in Europe and the U.S. have not been raided and closed down by counter-terrorism authorities."

But, he didn't write that. And if he had the knowledge to write it, he would not have dared to write it and file it. And if he had the integrity to write and file it, would the AP have accepted it? Is its motto "All the facts all the time"? Not likely.

That is giving Islam a good Western press. It is dishonest enough to cause one to develop a severe case of "media-phobia."

September 2007

Taking Islam Seriously

On the whole, I agreed with a recent Ayn Rand Institute op-ed, "The Terrorists' Motivation: Islam" (September 7, 2006), by Dr. Edwin Locke and Alex Epstein, and read it with great appreciation. Its principle point is that Islamic totalitarianism is a greater threat than most people can imagine. However, I had been saying that for years. I kept getting expressions of doubt concerning the fundamental nature of Islam, doubts that denied or questioned whether jihad against non-believers, infidels, and Western civilization in general was an integral weave of the Islamic cloth. These reservations and doubts came from some surprising Objectivist quarters.

But, going by recent observations by other Objectivists, I think no doubts remain among our number that Islam poses a mortal peril here and abroad. This is a positive way to mark the fifth anniversary of the Islamic attack on this country.

My only reservation about the op-ed can be found in this paragraph:

> "It is true that many Muslims who live in the West (like most Christians) reject religious fanaticism and are law-abiding and even loyal citizens, but this is because they have accepted some Western values, including respect for reason, a belief in individual rights, and the need for a separation between church and state. It is only to the extent that they depart from their religion - and from a society that imposes it - that they achieve prosperity, freedom, and peace."

Islam is just as insidiously corrupting as is Christianity. Name me one Christian who has a fundamental, unshakable respect for reason, individual rights, and a separation of church and state. True, as the op-ed points out, Christianity's "jihadist" character has been diluted since the Renaissance (and the recent resurgence of Christianity Harry Binswanger called an aberration). But most rank and file Christians are foggy on these ideas, while most of their "intellectual" spokesmen today are outspokenly hostile to them.

Islam cannot be tamed or diluted, not unless, as I've written elsewhere, the creed is gutted of its belligerent commandments. No Islamic scholar, ayatollah, or cleric is going to attempt that kind of "reformation" without risking a charge of apostasy and a fatwa on his life. If it were ever accomplished, what would be left would not be Islam, but a creed as innocuous and pacific as the Amish. The fundamental requirement of Islam is, simply put, abject, unquestioning submission by belief, conversion, or the sword (or bomb). It is as primitive and barbaric a creed as the Mayan or Aztec.

I am certain that if those American Muslims, who, as the op-ed describes in the op-ed, reject religious fanaticism and are law-abiding citizens, are ever faced with a choice, secularism or faith, they would side with faith. I see them as a fifth column here, kindling for the kind of warlike proselytizing that is common in mosques in Britain and Europe against the "host" country. We have seen the beginnings of such "radicalization" here as we've seen in Britain and Europe, with the SUV-jihadists and the Muslims who bought thousands of cell phones in a plot to destroy a Michigan bridge, and other incidents involving violent Muslim "activism."

What we have not seen here is any sincere, across-the-board condemnation of terrorism by Muslims by any American Muslim organization. Nor are we likely to. The creed forbids it; it would demand a conscious contradiction of principles. (And I'm not even including the transparent, pseudo-pious PR statements of CAIR or the Muslim Council of America, whose spokesmen have expressed a desire to see the Constitution replaced with Sharia law. CAIR, by the way, is an offshoot of Hamas and is more or less subsidized by Saudi Wahhabists.) Islam is not Episcopalism garbed in a hijab or burqa.

Furthermore, I don't think enough critics of Islam take seriously enough the "separatist" agenda of Islam in Western countries, a separatism or move to a status of "separate but equal" reminiscent of the black power movement of the 1960's and 1970's. The aforementioned Amish may wish to remain "separate" from American culture, and have largely done so, but they are not waging a jihadist campaign to convert other Americans or incorporate Amish principles into American law, either on the street or in court.

Just as a Christian must repudiate his creed in its entirety before he can begin to respect reason, endorse individual rights, and call for an iron curtain separation of church and state (most Christians adhere to these ideas more from "tradition" than from conscious conviction), so must a Muslim his. I think I understand Islam well enough to know that a repudiation of Islam, while necessary, is ethically and intellectually impossible to the non-thinking Muslim, and certainly impossible to Muslim clerics of any rank, who have a vested interest in enlarging their credulous congregations.

Anyone who was intellectually honest enough to attempt it would need to go into hiding, as did Wafa Sultan, the woman who condemned Islam on Al Jazeera TV, to elude her Muslim assassins. (Just the other day there was an item in the paper about a Sudanese editor who criticized Islam, who disappeared, and then was found dead on the outskirts of Khartoum, executed.) Briefly, I don't think it is possible for any Muslim to mentally compartmentalize his religious convictions as Christians and Jews do, or to think and act "outside the box." He is required to maintain his Islamic identity all his conscious hours. Christians or Jews can innovate in business, medicine, science and even the arts; I am not aware of any "Westernized" Muslim making a breakthrough in stem cell research or astrophysics or industrial production.

Finally, from a purely emotional standpoint, I find the presence of Muslims in the U.S. repulsive. There is no room in their creed for individualism, independence of mind, or for any of the virtues championed by Objectivism. Informally, I call them the "Borg," after the cybernetic invaders of the *Star Trek* science fiction series, the ultimate collectivist society of drones serving the "hive" in which there are no individuals and no individual minds. I cannot reconcile the thought of mosques in any part of the country with the images of Thomas Jefferson, Patrick Henry, and George Washington.

The image of Jefferson's statue in the Memorial rotunda next to the figure of a Muslim kneeling on a prayer mat in supplication to a fearsome ghost is too violently offensive. I refuse to ignore that contrast, nor will I accept it as a norm and shrug it off as unimportant.

Islam's means and ends are no less evil and inimical than the Borg's.

Islam represents a tyranny over men's minds incompatible with what this country was intended to be. Even in a semi-rational culture such as ours, there is no room for the *Koran* and *Hadith* and the Declaration of Independence and the Constitution in the same country or the same culture at the same time.

One could say this, as well, that ultimately there is no room in it for the *Bible* and the Declaration at the same time, either.

September 2006

The Current Administration

The Year of the Long Knives: Part I

Night of the Long Knives (June 30, 1934): Purge of Nazi leaders by Adolf Hitler. Fearing that the paramilitary SA ["Assault Division"] had become too powerful, Hitler ordered his elite SS [the paramilitary "Protective Echelon"] guards to murder the organization's leaders, including Ernst Rohm [head of the SA]. Also killed that night were hundreds of other perceived opponents of Hitler, including Kurt von Schleicher and Gregor Strasser. (*Britannica Concise Encyclopedia*)

Now that Barack Obama has unofficially won the Democratic presidential nomination, it is time to place this ambitious man under a microscope for closer examination. In a morbid sense, it has been instructive watching the two contending power lusters, Senator Hillary Clinton and Senator Obama, slash and gouge each other over what has seemed endless months of vying for the nomination, the one touting her alleged "experience" and the other touting his alleged political "innocence" and desire for "change."

So strong is their appetite for supreme political power that each has been willing to say anything, do anything, deny anything. Each has purged his campaign of supporters and workers and past associates, all of whom at various points in the primaries embarrassed the candidates or jeopardized their chances with the electorate and the party delegates.

And each has committed numerous memorable gaffes in speeches and off-the-record comments, gaffs that revealed either their ignorance of facts and of history and even of geography, or a willingness to lie in the rush to preserve a patina of veracity, experience, and trustworthiness.

Unlike the nocturnal bloodletting of the Nazis, the candidates' purgings have been public and bloodless and will continue to be that right up to the November national election. But, it will be purging nonetheless, all for the sake of maintaining images and stances of originality, wisdom and farsightedness. Obama has the most to purge. And unlike Rohm and Strasser, who charged Hitler with abandoning socialism in favor of a "personality cult," Obama will continue to purge anyone who provides substantive evidence that, beneath his glib but vapid rhetoric and blasé promises, he is promoting full-scale socialism, and that promoting it has always defined his political activism and ambition.

The "untouchables" are not completely cast out as liabilities, however, and will not mind the ostracism. They will simply stay out of sight until Obama thinks it opportune to invite them back into the open (if and when he wins the White House). It is important to remember that while Obama has "repudiated" them in nationally broadcast public ablutions, *they have not repudiated him.* Neither Rev. Jeremiah Wright nor Father Michael Pfleger has publicly cursed Obama for calling their ranting sermons "disgusting," nor has any black or white liberal supporter of Obama upbraided him for discarding the racist, rabble-rousing clerics.

This fact seems to have eluded his supporters and the news media, who are giddily eager to absolve him of any wrong-doing, misconduct, or having had a less than sterling past and political career. It is another form of Kennedy or Clinton idolization, one that sweeps all evidence of scandal, criminal behavior, and malfeasance beneath an impenetrable rug of irrelevancy. He makes us *feel* good, so never mind his missteps.

Why link an infamous chapter of Nazi history to any discussion of Barack Obama's character and political aspirations? Because the parallels of his rise in politics and that of Hitler's in Germany are too eerie in their particulars to ignore. To be sure, Obama's rise has been, in terms of violence, betrayal, and criminal skullduggery, entirely blameless. Never mind his early career as a "community" advocate, activist, and ward-heeler in Chicago and his somewhat lackluster but leftist record in the Illinois legislature and the U.S Senate. Obama himself is a man of no convictions, and a man of no convictions, as a consummate second-hander, will adopt the "greatest good for the greatest number" as his moral compass, whether or not he is running for office.

A man with no sense of self-identity will become what others wish him to be, or what he believes others wish him to be. The empty vessel will naturally gravitate to crowds to be filled to the brim with *their* hopes, dreams, wishes, sores and frustrations. Only then will he feel complete. He will become *their* servant, *their* icon, to be placed on an altar to be worshipped and prayed to in self-effacing idolatry.

So it is with Obama. It helps to explain why so many Americans are excited by him, and why he exudes a confidence not evident in any of the other candidates. His admirers cannot be excited by him because of his ideas; he has not expressed anything as solid as an idea (and clichés, bromides and populist tripe are not ideas), and his confidence grows as the number of his admirers and supporters grows.

Obama has not deliberately posed as a miracle-working Messiah who promises to cure all ills for all complainants; that is how his supporters and most of the news media view him, but he is willing to meet them halfway. And his race, fundamentally, is immaterial, regardless of what importance others attach to it. Virtually every other candidate has mouthed the same bromides, clichés, and populist tripe as Obama. Why they have worked for Obama and not much for anyone else (especially not for Hillary Clinton, whose sincerity is transparently phony and calculating) can be ascribed to his "charisma," his public speaking skills, and the apparent sincerity of the "feelings" behind his words.

Feelings. This is the key to understanding Obama's appeal. Ian Kershaw, noted biographer and professor at the University of Sheffield, wrote a two-volume biography of Hitler that is distinguished from other such biographies in that it not only dissects Hitler, but the German culture that made him possible, and indicts both. It is the only non-Objectivist biography of Hitler that comes near to Dr. Leonard Peikoff's *The Ominous Parallels: The End of Freedom in America* (1982) by offering a philosophical explanation for the Nazi phenomenon (it stops just short of reaching the same conclusions). Kershaw, in *Hitler, 1889-1936: Hubris* (1998), makes a number of important observations about how and why Hitler was able to succeed, first in rising through the tumultuous politics of the 1920's, then in seizing power with the approval of the political establishment and the electorate.

> "It was as a propagandist, not as an ideologue with a unique or special set of political ideas, that Hitler made his mark in these early years. There was nothing new, different, original, or distinctive about the ideas he was peddling in the Munich beerhalls. They were common currency among the various *völkisch* groups and sects and had already been advanced in all their essentials by the pre-war Pan-Germans. What Hitler did was to advertise unoriginal ideas in an original way. Others

could say the same thing but make no impact at all. It was less *what* he said, than *how* he said it that counted." ("The Beerhall Agitator," p. 133.)

Hillary Clinton can advocate "national unity," "change that matters," "working together," "social justice" and all the other unoriginal floating abstractions as often as can Obama, but make no lasting impression, because she has never been able to communicate sincerity. Obama can make that impression, especially when he couches those vague "yearnings" in what Saul Alinsky, the Chicago sometime communist community activist whom both Clinton and Obama have emulated in terms of applying his political tactics, called "middle class language." (Alinsky's influence on Clinton and Obama is discussed in my two articles on Rule of Reason, "Hillary Clinton's Uncle Ellsworth" and its "Postscript," August 8 and 10 respectively.)

In the contest for the Democratic nomination, Obama more successfully applied Alinsky's "principles" of political activism than did Clinton. Clinton has always talked *down* to her supporters and would-be voters; Obama talks *to* his supporters and would-be voters as an equal with many things in common with them. That is his subtle but no less calculating posture of camaraderie with the "oppressed" and "disenfranchised."

Kershaw shortly afterwards explains the confidence Hitler exuded.

"…[T]he response of the beerhall crowds – later the mass rallies – gave him the certainty, the self-assurance, the sense of security, which at this time he otherwise lacked."

Similarly, Obama almost glows when facing a wildly enthusiastic crowd. In one-on-one interviews with television reporters, however, he is soberingly banal and nondescript, almost as much as is Republican candidate John McCain.

Part Two of this commentary will examine the phenomenon of Obama's abrupt appearance on the national stage. The parallels there are also frighteningly eerie.

June 2008

The Year of the Long Knives: Part II

Discussing Adolf Hitler's rise from a "provincial hot-head and rabble-rouser" in the 1920's to his electrifying effect on "disaffected" Germans in *Hitler, 1889-1936: Hubris,* Ian Kershaw poses the paradox of how, among countless other "hot-heads" and "rabble-rousers" of the time, Hitler was so successful in establishing a rapport of anger and hatred, and then solves it at the same time:

> "This in itself suggests that what had changed above all was the milieu and context in which Hitler operated; that we should look in the first instance less to his own personality than to the motives and actions of those who came to be Hitler's supporters, admirers, and devotees – and not least his powerful backers – to explain his first breakthrough on the political scene. For what becomes clear – without falling into the mistake of presuming that he was no more than the puppet of the 'ruling classes' – is that Hitler would have remained a political nonentity without the patronage and support he obtained from influential circles in Bavaria. During this period, Hitler was seldom, if ever, master of his own destiny. The key decisions – to take over the party leadership in 1921, to engage the putsch adventure in 1923 – were not carefully conceived actions, but desperate forward moves to save face – behavior characteristic of Hitler to the end." (pp. 132-133)

Senator Barack Obama, former Illinois state senator, former senior lecturer at the University of Chicago Law School, and junior doyen of the Chicago welfare and community services machine, is also such a political nonentity – one of among dozens in the political spectrum who hanker for the limelight and the power – who could not have risen to the top of the Democratic Party establishment without the patronage, endorsement and support of influential circles within and outside the Party. It is because he is such a zero – a zero willing to be anything to all – that he was picked, groomed and promoted to run for the office of President of the United States. Regardless of the image Obama projects, that of an independent force master of his own destiny – and it is a manufactured image, to be sure – it is the nature of modern American politics that he could not have moved a single square on that chessboard without being covered by more powerful pieces.

Why would he among all those others be chosen to become the point man for the collectivist movements that wish to take full control of the country? Because he is malleable, chimerical, and can be virtually anything to anyone who claims to be a victim of something. Also, he has demonstrated his ability to overcome his many liabilities with the cooperation of a fawning news media.

For one thing, he is deceitful. He has denied being a Muslim and has emphasized his Christian background, or has alternately downplayed his youthful Muslim studies. Well, according to Islam, once a Muslim, always a Muslim, even in a state of apostasy, even if one converts to another faith but retains the full name of Barack Hussein Mohammed Obama.

But, this is not important. What is important is that he thinks it is enough of a liability that he is willing to fudge on the truth. Daniel Pipes discusses in detail Obama's religious background in a *FrontPage* article of April 29, "Barack Obama's Muslim Childhood."

Another liability is his family history. He is obviously of mixed racial parentage, but that is neither here nor there. Also irrelevant is whether or not his mother, "Stanley" Ann Dunham, and his father, Barack Obama Sr., were ever married in Hawaii or elsewhere. There is a record of their divorce (Obama Sr. left Ann and Barack to pursue a degree at Harvard, and then returned to Kenya) but no record of their marriage.

Barack Junior's mother later married Lolo Soetoro, an Indonesian oil manager and practicing Muslim, which accounts for Obama's time in Jakarta. They were divorced in the late 1970s. Obama has a half-sister, Maya, of whom nothing has ever been said by him, but he has "advertised" his relatives in Kenya.

Obama has claimed that his mother was the daughter of a conservative Methodist or Baptist family from Kansas. However, her parents were left-wingers whose Unitarian church near Seattle was so sympathetic to communism that it was nicknamed "the little red church."

Obama's mother also attended a high school near Seattle that was notorious enough to be investigated by the House Un-American Activities Subcommittee for its connections to the American Communist Party. Here Ann Dunham absorbed literature-destroying "critical theory" and Karl Marx, and was so influenced by the leftist curriculum that she became and remained a radical leftist. Doubtless young Barack was exposed at home to nothing but his mother's political opinions, in addition to "black" history and "black" literature. It would account for his knee-jerk collectivist rhetoric. And, it would not be much of a stretch of the imagination to suppose that, had Ann Dunham ever attended stateside universities, she might have become a member of the Students for a Democratic Society or the Weather Underground. But, see her "public service" career here.

She would have been old enough and "revolutionary" enough to join the likes of Mark Rudd, the SDS or Bill Ayers and Bernadine Dohrn of the Weather Underground. Doubtless she cheered them on from afar as they protested the Vietnam War, brought anarchy to America's streets with demonstrations, and eventually turned to terrorist bombings of the Capitol building, the Pentagon, and the State Department.

She did not get to meet Ayers and Dohrn, two of the Weathermen terrorists yet to be charged with the bombing murder of a San Francisco policeman, but her son "Barry" did. They are friends of his and pillars of Chicago's left-liberal establishment, Ayers a "distinguished professor" of education at the University of Illinois at Chicago and sometime education advisor to Mayor Richard Daley, Dohrn associate professor of law at Northwestern University School of Law and director of Northwestern's Children and Family Justice Center.

Ayers still serves on the board of the Woods Fund, a Chicago-based charity that develops community groups to help the poor (echoes of Saul Alinsky again), as had Obama for nine years until 2002. Ayers, however, claims Obama, is just "a guy who lives in my neighborhood." Ayers promoted Obama in a 1995 fundraiser when he ran for the state senate. Nice neighbors if you can get them.

Obama complained when someone brought up his close association with Ayers that "the notion that somehow as a consequence of me knowing somebody who engaged in detestable acts 40 years ago when I was 8 years old, somehow reflects on me and my values, doesn't make much sense." Well, yes, it does make sense. Ayers and Dohrn should have served hard time for their actions, just as Ted Kennedy, now the patriarch of the American Borgias, should have served hard time for manslaughter. Both Obama and Hillary Clinton have a penchant for having close "associations" with lawbreakers who later teach law and justice or become lawmakers.

Obama was a close friend and political crony of Alice Palmer, a black Illinois state senator from 1990 to 1995, and an open admirer of the Soviet Union who served on the board of the World Peace Council, a Soviet front. Obama, Ayers, and Dohrn often attended political meetings at Palmer's Chicago home. Just "neighbors."

(Hillary Clinton also has radical terrorist skeletons rattling in one of her many scandal-stuffed closets, the ones whose criminal sentences her husband commuted in his last days of office, before they both made off with the White House silverware and other public valuables – but that's another story.)

After he had unofficially won the Democratic race for the nomination, on June 4 Obama broadcast a message of triumph to his supporters, which said, among other things:

> "It's going to take hard work, but thanks to you and millions of other donors and volunteers, no one has ever been more prepared for such a challenge."

Prepared, that is, "to turn the page on the policies of the past and bring new energy and new ideas to the challenges we face…This is our moment. This is our time." Obama's chief deceit is that he is just a clean-cut knock-off of John F. Kennedy of yore, loaded with good intentions and plausible-sounding solutions to everything.

Prepared? Michelle Malkin, in "Barack Obama: Gaffe Machine" (May 21, 2008), cites some instances of just how ill-prepared Obama is. Click here for a measure of his wisdom and respect for the truth. Did you know there were fifty-seven states in the union? That his parents were inspired to conceive him because of the Bloody Sunday March in Selma, Alabama in 1965, even though he was born in 1961? And that Obama cited a Life Magazine article he saw at the age of nine, whose photographs caused his "racial awakening." Malkin reports, "In fact, the Life article and the photographs don't exist, say the magazine's own historians."

One of British playwright Terence Rattigan's early plays was a satire on Hitler, *Follow My Leader*. Unfortunately, what is happening in America today is not satire. Barack Obama wishes the country to follow his lead. Regrettably, there are too many Americans ready and willing to.

Part Three of this commentary will delve into Obama's political "angels."

June 2008

The Year of the Long Knives: Part III

D escribing the political climate of Weimar Germany in *Hitler, 1889-1936: Hubris,* Ian Kershaw notes that Germany was "a Republic without republicans." One could just as well say that of the United States today, our republicans being of the intellectual and moral caliber of the Founders but who are entirely absent from the modern American political universe. No politician today advocates life, liberty, property and the pursuit of happiness; the Declaration of Independence and the original Constitution, *sans* the statist amendments to it, may as well be indecipherable Turkish runes.

A friend noted that while the Democrats wish to destroy the American Revolution, the Republicans seem to have forgotten it ever happened, which explains not only why they have never been able to defend it, but have been complicit in its steady destruction. Republican presidential candidate John McCain is not any kind of reactionary alternative to Barack Obama. If the current political environment can be likened to a coin, then heads it is altruist, tails it is collectivist, and McCain is simply the ridged edge on its side.

Noting the appeal of Hitler early in his career, Kershaw writes:

> "The crowds that began to flock in 1919 and 1920 to Hitler's speeches were not motivated by refined theories. For them, simple slogans, kindling the fires of anger, resentment, and hatred, were what worked. But what they were offered in the Munich beerhalls was nevertheless a vulgarized version of ideas which were in far wider circulation." (p. 137)

Ideas, however, notes Kershaw, "held no interest for Hitler as abstractions. They were important to him only as tools of mobilization."

To date, has there been any measurable difference between that and what has passed for "debate" between any of the current presidential candidates? Other than the usual bromides, clichés, and populist tripe widely circulated in our schools, the news media, and in the culture in general (e.g., universal health care, taxing corporate profits, "fighting" global warming), has Clinton, Obama or McCain enunciated a single *idea*?

I challenge anyone to find any *substance* in the following excerpts from Obama's speech to Virginia's Jefferson-Jackson Dinner in Richmond, on February 9:

"Each of us running for the Democratic nomination agrees on one thing that the other party does not – the next President must end the disastrous policies of George W. Bush. And both Senator Clinton and I have put forth detailed plans and good ideas that would do just that."

What policies of Bush have been disastrous? What detailed plans and good ideas would end them? Would more controls and regulations of the economy correct Bush's and Congress's controls and regulations? Would the Democrats have fought the "war on terror" any differently from the Republicans? Would our foreign policy have meant more or less appeasement of our committed enemies? As Ayn Rand would put it: Blank out.

"But I am running for President because I believe that to actually make change happen – to make this time different than [*sic*] all the rest – we need a leader who can finally move beyond the divisive politics of Washington and bring Democrats, Independents, and Republicans together to get things done. That's how we'll win this election, and that's how we'll change this country when I am President of the United States."

What change? Isn't "divisive" politics a *good* thing, as opposed to one-party rule with no dissension or opposition permitted? Is everyone supposed to put aside his principles and convictions and mobilize for "national unity"? In all of his rhetoric, Obama employs the same appeal to *emotion* that Hitler employed all throughout *his* career. The similarities are spine-tinglingly ominous: Kershaw writes:

"While Hitler basically appealed to *negative* feelings – anger, resentment, hatred – there was also a 'positive' element in the proposed remedy to the proclaimed ills. However platitudinous, the appeal to restoration of liberty through national unity, the need to work together of 'workers of the brain and hand,' the social harmony of a 'national community,' and the protection of the 'little man' through the crushing of his exploiters, were, to go from the applause they invariably produced, undeniably attractive propositions to Hitler's audiences. And Hitler's own passion and fervor successfully conveyed the message – to those already predisposed to it – that no other way was possible, that Germany's revival would and could be brought about; and that it lay in the power of ordinary Germans to make it happen through their own struggle, sacrifice, and will. The effect was more that of a religious revivalist meeting than a normal political gathering." (p. 150, *Italics* mine)

There are no substantive differences between Obama's rhetoric and Hitler's. Or even between Hillary Clinton's and Hitler's. Hillary also views society as an organic whole ripe for "remodeling." All three regard the individual as a part of that "social organism" who would be permitted his few peccadilloes but otherwise answerable to society or the State. Substitute a few appropriate words, and Kershaw's description could just as well be of Obama's rhetorical technique.

Are not many voters drawn to Obama's "passion and fervor," are they not "predisposed" to "change," do they not want to help "make it happen"? Have so many been brainwashed and indoctrinated into believing they are "little" enough to deserve the protection and guidance of the state? Is listening to Obama a form of religious "rapture"? As for the "restoration of liberty," what the Germans got in exchange for "helping to make it happen" certainly was not liberty. Doubtless the concept of liberty is as empty and meaningless to Obama as it was to Hitler (as it was to countless Germans).

Senator Ted Kennedy wielded his own "long knife" and stabbed Hillary Clinton in the back by endorsing Obama. Unless one thought this was Kennedy's perverted way of bolstering Clinton's chances, his knowing that his endorsement was the kiss of death – given Kennedy's known reputation for collectivist elitism, venality and corruption – the endorsement made sense. If there was one way he could punish America for not going socialist at his beck and call, it was to back the man he believes could deliver on that vengeance. Kennedy's endorsement was a major signal to other prominent Democrats that they should follow suit. And they did.

Another "kiss of death" endorsement came from ailing Fidel Castro of Communist Cuba. In a newspaper column he stated that he had "no personal rancor" toward Obama, but "if I defended him I would do a huge favor for his adversaries." Shrewd policy. Keep the cat in the bag.

Yet another "kiss of death" endorsement came from Ahmed Yousef, a political advisor to Hamas, the terrorist organization and now government of the Palestinians, who last month opined:

> "We like Mr. Obama and hope that he will win the election. I do believe that Mr. Obama is like John Kennedy, a great man with great principles. He has a vision to change America, to

make it in a position to lead the world community, but not with domination and arrogance."

None of these dubious endorsements has troubled Obama, the news media, or the Ivy League. One large segment of the American population that finds Obama just as compelling and attractive is academia. There are few "republicans" in this venue, but plenty of Marxists, existentialists, left-liberals, deconstructionists, and multiculturalists who also condemn the U.S.'s "domination and arrogance," and the U.S. as a free country as a matter of habit.

"Barack Obama appears to be winning the faculty lounge straw poll – his presidential campaign is cultivating academics and pacing the field in collecting cash from them," reported the *Politico* site last August in a report, "Professors have a crush on Obama."

"Obama, whose website features an 'Academics for Obama' page, raised nearly $1.5 million in the first half of the year [2007] from people who work for colleges and universities, according to an analysis of campaign finance data by the nonpartisan Center for Responsive Politics."

In the *Politico* report, Larry Sabato, a University of Virginia political science professor, said that Obama seems to have "a special appeal among academics, particularly those at four-year institutions. Even at places like UVA, which are more conservative than most, it's overwhelmingly Obama."

Sabato went on to explain that the Democrats can always count on academics to contribute money and to vote the straight Party ticket, and so are not courted as vigorously as are wealthy donors.

On April 2, Michael Barone, a political commentator, in an exhaustive analysis of the Democratic primaries, "In Terms of Geography, Obama Appeals to Academics and Clinton Appeals to Jacksonians," provided a clue to why academics are so reliable:

"Academics and public employees (and of course many, perhaps most, academics in the United States are public employees) love the arts of peace and hate the demands of war. Economically, defense spending competes for the public-sector dollars that academics and public employees think are rightfully their own. More important, I think, warriors are competitors for the honor that academics and public employees think rightfully belongs to them."

There is no need to burden most American academics with "refined theories," either. They will settle for a vulgar slogan over a syllogism any day. They are already committed to "remodeling" and "changing" America, and have been imparting those imperatives to students for decades. Barack Obama was one of those students.

The fourth and final fourth part of this commentary will focus on the capitalist "big money" behind Obama.

June 2008

The Year of the Long Knives: Part IV

The knives came out and flashed to sink into the very fresh corpse of Hillary Clinton's bid for the presidency. The occasion was the National Conference for Media Reform in Minneapolis on June 7. According to Cliff Kincaid, writing for *Accuracy in Media* on June 8, the conference was more a "Barack Obama for President rally" than a conference.

> "Several speakers, including Federal Communications Commissioner Michael Copps, used the Obama campaign slogan, 'Yes, we can,' as they urged the thousands of 'progressives' in the audience to bring 'change' to Washington, D.C."

Clinton's offense was having voted for the war in Iraq. Also, she is perceived by the far-lefties attending the conference as a part of the Washington establishment they believe Obama wants to "change." The fact that she conceded defeat and endorsed Obama in the name of party unity counted for nothing with many of the conference speakers.

> "Meanwhile, a Canadian, Naomi Klein, who writes for the *British Guardian* and *The Nation* magazine, told the conference that Hillary Clinton's endorsement of Obama was 'a partial victory for the forum gathered here tonight.' She said that Clinton was the candidate of the establishment and that her 'coronation' had been derailed….Referring to Clinton's loss, Klein said, 'Somebody paid a price (for Iraq) at last.'"

From all appearances, however, the criticisms of Clinton were mere rationalizations of resentment that she was not left-wing enough. The attendees preferred Obama because he is as far left as anyone could get without being the nominee from Communist Cuba.

Kincaid might have subtitled his report, "They Smell Blood." While Clinton earnestly wishes to enslave the medical profession and shackle all Americans to universal health care (as does Obama, else why would Ted Kennedy endorse him?), the "progressives" at the Media Reform conference wish to sink their shivs into the First Amendment and shackle American minds. Obama as president, they believe, will be completely amenable to such a policy, and there is no reason to doubt their confidence in him. (In a premonitory echo of how the would-be wardens of our minds will seek to scuttle freedom of speech, see Adam Liptak's June 12th article, "Unlike Others, U.S. Defends Freedom to Offend in Speech," in The New York Times.)

Kincaid errs when he claims that "media reform," such as disinterring the so-called Fairness Doctrine, would target conservatives and Republicans exclusively for statutory gagging. The gauleiters of the various tribes and warring factions and the judicial sensitivity police would gag everyone but the politically correct.

"'It's time to put a cop back on the beat,' demanded Democratic FCC commissioner Copps, in framing the 'media reform' debate. With Obama in the White House, Democrats would have a majority on the commission," and the new chairman of the commission would be an Obama appointee. Couple that with the predicted majorities of Democrats in both houses of Congress, and *de facto* censorship would be guaranteed (besides much other horrific socialist legislation; see FrontPageMagazine's "The Democrats' Platform for Revolution" of May 5).

> "As they see it, of course, the 'cop' on the beat is going to be the FCC, regulating and dictating media ownership rules, enforcing broadcaster compliance with the 'public interest,' and control over the flow of news and information over the Internet. The latter is euphemistically and misleadingly called 'net neutrality' or 'Internet freedom.'"

The fine-print catch is that federal regulation of the Internet (or of any venue of speech or expression) would be, in practice, neither "neutral" nor "free." Yahoo, Google, Microsoft, and other "public" Internet carriers already cooperate with totalitarian governments in limiting or blocking access to the Internet. How much resistance do you think they would offer a "changed" Washington against performing the same policing service in the U.S.?

> "Klein, a critic of what she calls 'disaster capitalism,' said that Obama's support from Wall Street financial interests was a problem and griped that Democrats, rather than Republicans, were now getting more campaign dollars from the 'arms industry.'"

She and her appreciative audience also want Obama to get the U.S. out of Iraq now, and to create a "Green New Deal."

Which brings us to Wall Street and the support its denizens are giving Obama. The *AIM* article reveals:

"The 'media reform' movement has been funded by
Democratic moneybags George Soros, a billionaire and
convicted inside trader, and liberal foundations such as the
Wallace Global Fund, named for FDR's pro-communist Vice
President Henry Wallace."

Unlike Bill Gates and Warren Buffet, who have elected to perform
penance for their financial success by pouring their fortunes into the
bottomless pits of altruist humanitarianism with the conscious, stated
goal of dissolving their wealth, Soros is actively funding by the
millions of dollars the conversion of this country from a semi-free
welfare state into a full-scale, totalitarian one. Given the rabid,
virulently anti-freedom, anti-man, anti-capitalist nature of the
organizations he subsidizes (and which would not exist but for his
money), such as MoveOn and Media Matters, such behavior cannot
stem from anything but a burning malice. He is their chief "angel" and
Barack Obama's major financial enabler.

Soros calls the U.S. "fascist," and has likened President Bush to
Hitler, but it is fascism his so-called philanthropy is fueling in the U.S.
If one reads his biography or any of his political books, it would appear
that he does not know the difference the Nazism he survived in
Hungary and the communism he escaped in 1947. Or rather, he
disapproves of tyranny imposed by one country on another, but an
indigenous democratic tyranny receives his blessing. If the "people"
vote for it, then it must be okay.

The Investor's Business Daily (IBD) on September 20, 2007, ran
an excellent exposé on Soros, "George Soros: The Man, the Mind and
the Money Behind MoveOn." About the man who boasts of giving
away $400 million a year, it stresses that:

"He calls himself a philanthropist and has given away $5
billion of his now $8.5 billion fortune through his principal
vehicle, the Open Society Institute. The institute, in turn, has
passed cash on to far more radical groups, such as
MoveOn.org."

"He has handed $3.1 million to the left-wing Tides
Foundation, which funds organizations such as the Sea
Shepherds, Earth First! and the Ruckus Society, that have
condoned or engaged in eco-terrorism."

"He also gave at least $150,000 to ACORN (the Association of
Community Organizations for Reform Now), the left-wing

group best known for pushing minimum wage hikes, for illegal-immigrant amnesty and harassing Wal-Mart."

"Soros additionally finances groups best described as helpful to terrorists. Since 1998, he has given the American Civil Liberties Union $5 million to empower criminals, including lawsuits on behalf of terrorists' 'civil rights.' Soros' Open Society Institute gave $20,000 for the legal defense of radical attorney Lynne Stewart. She was convicted in 2002 of abetting jailed terrorists after the 1993 World Trade Center bombing."

In one of its closing remarks, the IBD editorial concludes:

"…[P]ick any cause that seeks to weaken the U.S. and it's not hard to find Soros' name on its list of financial backers. Most of these causes are financed by relatively small amounts, but that's all that's needed to make trouble. And without the cash, countless bad ideas would have no presence in American political debate at all."

Nor would there be any Barack Obamas to tout such bad ideas with a "passion" and "sincerity" that disguises their fundamental evil. Obama would have no presence in that debate if it were not for the gifts that keep on hurting the U.S. from the likes of Soros.

Naomi Klein need not worry that support for Obama by Wall Street financial interests will corrupt her messiah. A man with no first-hand convictions, or who is a patchwork quilt of second-hand beliefs, can be influenced, but not corrupted. How can one corrupt a vacuum? And George Soros is not Obama's only enabler.

A New York Magazine article of April 16, 2007, "Money Chooses Sides," reveals the kinds of men and their money who have funded the Obama and Clinton campaigns. It drools over the pecking order of fund-raisers among the wealthy and the politically connected, in a sliding scale that begins with Soros and descends to the mere millionaires. Most of them are investment bankers, hedge fund managers, or executives of financial institutions. The article focuses on Obama's and Clinton's efforts to raise enough to fund their primary campaigns.

It is a disgusting exposé of the low caliber of men – every one of them a people-oriented, amoral pragmatist – who would loose a dictator on the country without a second thought. Most of the men who are willing to donate to Obama's campaign or work to raise millions for it do it because Obama makes them *feel* good. He's against the war in Iraq, he's for "change," he's for "elevating" the tone of politics. Not once in the entire article does any one of them express an *idea*.

The New York Magazine article offers several portraits. Here is one of Robert Wolf, CEO of UBS Americas:

> "What Wolf, 45, was looking for was a candidate who could change the tenor of our politics. 'I'd like my children to soon see a president give a State of the Union address and have both parties applaud,' he tells me. But Wolf was looking, too, for a campaign where his presence would be 'impactful,' for a candidate who would take his calls, listen to his ideas. *He wanted to feel the love.* And while Wolf refuses to speak ill of Clinton, it's clear he doubted that, no matter how much dough he raised, he'd ever be feeling it from her." (*Italics* mine.)

> When Wolf had a private dinner with Obama, Wolf gushed: "I felt so honored to be sitting down with him for two hours on an occasion like that [when Bush announced the troop surge in Iraq.], knowing that he was going off to be interviewed on television later."

Translation: "The rock-star messiah touched me! He deigned to dine with me! He loves me! He won't hurt me when he's in office!"

Wolf might sing a different song if Obama and his "changed" Washington decide that the government should regulate all commercial investments and speculation. Hitler "loved" his industrialist and banking supporters, too, but, as Leonard Peikoff notes in *The Ominous Parallels: The End of Freedom in America*, he proceeded to fit them with the fetters of National Socialism when he assumed power. (See p. 247, Stein & Day hardcover.) I say *might*, because Wolf and his fund-raising colleagues, including George Soros, may on the other hand feel very comfortable with the arrangement.

Comfortable, but keeping a wary eye out for the long knife that is always, and necessarily – given the nature of power politics – somewhere behind someone's back, one reserved especially for friends, supporters, and other useful and thoughtless idiots.

June 2008

The Year of the Long Knives: A Postscript

Here are some observations I did not think appropriate to include in Part IV of these commentaries on Barack Obama, or which I omitted for length considerations.

In the New York Magazine article, "Money Chooses Sides" (April 15th, 2007) note the composition of the photograph that accompanies it. I do not think it is accidental. I do not know if the photographer (or even Obama himself) intended the tableau, but of all the pictures doubtless taken of the event, this was the one selected by the magazine's editors to illustrate Obama's influence. Their motive may have been mockery of the guests or unintended adulation of Obama. That is irrelevant. The picture captures the essence of Obama's appeal.

Obama seems to descend the stairs, microphone in hand, looking very preacherly as he brings the "gospel" to the mortals below. All the mortals gape up at him with undisguised worship, as though he were indeed a messiah or savior, and are hanging on his every word. Remember that these are all Park and Fifth Avenue millionaires there by RSVP. A good political cartoonist could render the photograph to show Obama in Moses-like robes, one hand raised with an instructive finger pointed in the air, the other arm cradling two stone tablets with the Ten Commandments of socialism (the words, however, would be fuzzy and nearly illegible).

The only person *not* gaping at Obama is George Soros, seated directly behind Obama's left. He looks vaguely bored but also smugly content with what he is hearing and with the undivided attention of the other guests.

Then, another point I did not dwell on, for I wished to leave the reader to make his own inferences, is why so many wealthy people are throwing their money and support behind Obama. Basically, and this is connected to his making them *feel good*, it is a form of penance for and expiation of the "sin" of wealth, not unlike that being performed by Bill Gates and Warren Buffet. This picture was taken long before Obama "resigned" from Jeremiah Wright's church, but one cannot help but suspect that he and his campaign managers were consciously but subtly instituting the Obama Church of Hope, Change, and Salvation.

I end this postscript with a brief excerpt from *Book II: Hugh Kenrick*, of the *Sparrowhawk* series (pp. 115-116). Political and charity events to raise money from the wealthy and the politically influential are nothing new. The place is London, the time, 1755:

....Bucklad House had undergone lengthy renovations, and the Pumphretts wished to mark their completion with a concert, to which were invited a list of London worthies. Lady Chloe, wife of Sir Henoch Pannell...was the mover behind this event. A donation of five guineas per person was levied, the receipts to be given to Lady Chloe's own organization, the Westminster Charity for London Waifs. "She's doing her penance early," confided Sir Henoch with sly derision to friends in the Commons who had been invited to the concert, "so that she may enjoy the rest of the season without the encumbrance of conscience. She is essentially a *moral* woman...."

June 2008

Follow Our Leader

The Muezzin of Pennsylvania Avenue (President Barack Obama) sang in his semi-mellifluous voice. American business leaders answered his call to prayers and bowed to the god of pragmatism.

Like British playwright Terence Rattigan's infuriatingly unpublished play, *Follow My Leader* (1940), a satiric attack on Nazi Germany, the true substance of President Barack Obama's December 15th meeting with twenty American business leaders at Blair House in Washington must remain unknown to most Americans. Aside from what has been reported in newspapers that certain topics were discussed and that attendees "felt good" about the gathering, no one knows what Obama said to these individuals that mattered, or what they said to him. What was the nature of those discussions? Was it an invitation to attend this meeting, or a command? Or do Obama and the attendees treat the terms as synonymous?

The Washington Post reported some significant absentees, major bank executives, with the exception of Robert Wolf, president of the financial services firm UBS. This is the company that cooperated with the Internal Revenue Service to uncover the identities and assets of some 15,000 secret account holders who thought their money was safe from government confiscation.

> No major U.S. bank executives came, even though the financial industry has had an especially rocky relationship with the White House after the passage of financial overhaul legislation and the president's criticism of "fat cat" bankers. The administration has tried to build a rapport with executives such as Jamie Dimon of J.P. Morgan Chase and Brian Moynihan of Bank of America, neither of whom attended the meeting.

> Also missing was Ivan Seidenberg, chief executive of Verizon, who delivered a stinging speech in June, saying the president's policies hurt economic growth. Seidenberg, who is also chairman of the Business Roundtable, presented a "road map" last week of policies supported by the business community relating to taxes, trade and energy.

Also missing was someone with the capacity for "spontaneous" anger of South Carolina representative Joe Wilson. I am betting that no one at this prayer meeting had the *chutzpah* to reply to the muezzin, "You lie!"

According to the Los Angeles Times, Wolf said afterward that it was "a very constructive, positive meeting." Which means nothing. "Constructive," in what sense? "Positive," how? You fill in the blanks. Many of the attendees were ardent Obamites.

> The group consisted of some strong Obama supporters —
> Google chief Eric Schmidt, Silicon Valley venture capitalist
> John Doerr and Chicago billionaire Penny Pritzker — along
> with such corporate leaders as John Chambers from Cisco,
> Jeffrey Immelt from GE, Indra Nooyi from PepsiCo Inc., Paul
> Otellini from Intel Corp. and Brian Roberts from Comcast.

Unless someone releases a transcript of who said what during the meeting, the country must be satisfied with the unfounded assumption that the participants, including the White House, were not discussing how better to further nationalize the economy. The Washington Post's Perry Bacon wrote:

> In a session with 20 chief executives…Obama - whose sharp
> rhetoric about pay on Wall Street has annoyed some executives
> - declared, "I want to dispel any notion we want to inhibit your
> success," according to a source in the room.

Also in attendance at prayers were executives from Honeywell International, United Parcel Service, Eli Lily & Co., Boeing, Comcast, Motorola, Centerbridge Partners, and American Express. Prayer, after all, is nothing more than earnest wishful thinking with a dash of hope, of blanking out reality and squeezing one's eyes shut, thinking, "Please, let it be! (or not)."

Dana Milbank, a regular columnist for The Washington Post, let the cat out of the bag with the title of his December 15th column, "The socialist president plays host to capitalism." Writing with an obvious bitter sarcasm directed at Obama, Milbank ascribes the appellation "socialist" to "many Republicans," but it is an honest appraisal of Obama's ideological identity and a confession of Milbank's political persuasion. He, too, wondered what was actually said during the meeting by all the parties.

> Whatever Obama said privately to the executives over the next
> four-plus hours, they must have liked it. When they emerged
> from Blair House, several of them stopped at the microphones

to welcome the president into the club of capitalists. "I think they have a lot of business acumen in the White House," judged UBS's Robert Wolf, an Obama golfing partner.

That was worse than saying nothing. "They" in the White House have the business acumen of Bernie Madoff, now serving a life sentence at the Butner Federal Correctional Complex near Raleigh, North Carolina for his multi-billion dollar Ponzi scheme. If that is Wolf's honest assessment of the Obama administration's notion of business, it would be advisable to avoid doing business with UBS.

The Blair House meeting is just the latest in a succession of meetings between Obama and business leaders to ease tensions between him and the leaders of our alleged free market system. This one was supposed to help patch things up in the aftermath of the midterm elections. Aside from saying prayers and speaking in tongues (to the press and the public), the business leaders also performed ablutions.

> Jim McNerney, president and chief executive of Boeing, said after the meeting, "We have a chance for a new beginning." McNerney later told CNBC: "We all made our apologies and said we wanted to move on."

To what? The president gave little indication.

> President Barack Obama said he and 20 company executives made "good progress" during a four and a half hour meeting toward establishing closer cooperation between government and business to accelerate the U.S. economic recovery. "We focused on jobs and investment, and they feel optimistic that by working together we can get some of that cash off the sidelines," Obama said as he left the session yesterday, referring to the almost $2 trillion that he said companies have amassed.

Cooperation and collaboration to accomplish what? Since when do corporate executives seek the advice of the government on how to invest their companies' money? One supposes the answer is when private individuals regard the government as the lodestone of their purposes. Since when do presidents feel they have the right to advise private individuals on how to conduct their business? When those individuals grant him the sanction to "guide" them.

Honeywell chairman David Cote said, after the meeting,

Executives at the meeting agreed with the president's assessment that the two sides made progress. "It's important for business and government to be able to work together," Cote said. "I came away feeling very good."

What can explain this secular version of Islamic submission to the American version of Louis IV, the Sun King? Gerald F. Seib wrote about a similar "rapprochement" between the White House and business last February, in The Wall Street Journal. Commenting on the ablutions performed by the U.S. Chamber of Commerce after its previous harsh criticisms of White House economic and social policies, he noted that Obama's signals of reconciliation were merely rhetorical.

The president who somewhat famously told Republicans earlier in the week, "I am not an ideologue," told his party's senators they shouldn't be ideologues either. "We've got to be non-ideological about our approach to these things. We've got to make sure that our party understands that, like it or not, we have to have a financial system that is healthy and functioning, so we can't be demonizing every bank out there," Mr. Obama said.

One would be right to feel a sense of *déjà vu*, when, on December 7th, he replied to liberal and Democratic critics who upbraided him for "compromising" over extending the Bush tax cuts for two years.

Obama's tone was alternately defensive and fiery. He dismissed his Democratic critics as "sanctimonious" and obsessed with staking out a "purist position." He said they hold views so unrealistic that, by their measure of success, "we will never get anything done."

And what is the difference between an *ideologue* and an ideological *purist?* Not a whit.

Clearly, the business leaders who answered the call to prayers are "non-ideological" pragmatists, empty vessels – many of them, except for those committed to the White House agenda. It is their muezzin who, contrary to his assertions notwithstanding, is the purist and ideologue. And yet, critics and congratulators are proclaiming that he is now a "centrist."

The centrist label is wholly unjustified, warned Charles Krauthammer, the Washington Post columnist who has so often and accurately kenned Obama's soul, style, and savvy. In his December 17th column, "The new comeback kid," he notes:

> ...[S]ome on the right are gloating that Obama had been maneuvered into forfeiting his liberal base. Nonsense. He will never lose his base. Where do they go? Liberals will never have a president as ideologically kindred – and they know it. For the left, Obama is as good as it gets in a country that is barely 20 percent liberal. The conservative gloaters were simply fooled again by the flapping and squawking that liberals ritually engage in before folding at Obama's feet.

American business leaders, most of them, will continue to follow their leader, together with their enemies, the liberals and the left. From this point on, on up through the presidential race of 2012, there will be many more calls to prayer from Pennsylvania Avenue.

December 2010

The Bill of Rights
(National Archives)

Freedom of Speech

Ashes for Allah: New Calls for Censorship

In the 21st century, on the lunatic fringe of American religion, a man decided to revive the medieval practice of putting an animal or inanimate object on trial for some grave offense, which was usually for witchcraft or being an instrument of the devil. The medievalist man is Terry Jones, pastor of the Dove Outreach Center in Gainesville, Florida, who announced plans to hold a "trial" of the Islamic *Koran*, charging it with "inciting murder, rape and terrorism." Mr. Jones's capacity for intellectual discourse on the evil of the ideas contained in the book being severely limited (he is a Baptist), burning an inanimate object was all that is left to him in the way of rebuttal and protest.

> On the evening of March 20, the "trial" went ahead with Jones presiding. It ended with another pastor setting alight a kerosene-soaked copy of the Qur'an.
>
> A brief Agence France Presse (AFP) report said that although the event was open to the public fewer than 30 people attended. A subsequent local media report said the only journalists who turned up on the day were an AFP stringer, several students and an unassigned photographer. A video clip was posted online, however.

The news media paid the event little or no attention. Jones had promised to burn a copy of the Koran last September 11, on the anniversary of 9/11, but was talked out of it by officials who feared a repetition of the Danish Mohammad cartoon riots. They feared in vain.

The riots occurred anyway. For Muslims, knowledge is a dangerous thing. If it doesn't fit, they throw a fit.

Everyone underestimated the determination of Jones to make some statement, however addled it might be, and presumed that his apparent thirst for publicity had been slaked.

The "trial" served as an excuse for another round of riots, murder and mayhem by Muslims. Warring Muslim factions, however, have burned or destroyed more copies of the Koran than have any group of Westerners, but this fact is an unthinkable thought to Muslims. As with Jones's original broadcast intention to burn a copy of the Koran, together with the publication of the Danish cartoons, there was also this time a measurable delayed reaction that went unnoticed. Time passed between knowledge of the "offenses" and Muslim reaction. This was to give the doyens of "anger management" time to whip their predisposed flocks and armies of manqués into a frenzy.

As of April 5th, the riots and protests against Jones and a potpourri of things Western continue.

A unique train of events ensued, one that led to the latest blathering of American politicians.

> Afghan President Hamid Karzai, who last week drew Afghan public attention to the burning, an event that initially gained little media coverage, on Sunday called on the U.S. Houses of Congress to join in the condemnation and prevent a repeat incident.

Several Muslim clerics seized on this unsolicited piece of Constitutional advice by our alleged "ally" to give their humble congregations double doses of feverish outrage.

Karzai was abetted in this by Pakistan.

> On March 22, Pakistan President Asif Ali Zardari, in a speech to the federal parliament, condemned the incident "in the strongest possible words," and Pakistan's foreign ministry called the burning a "despicable act." Dozens of reports on the Qur'an burning appeared in Pakistani media outlets on March 22-23, but the story received negligible coverage elsewhere in the Islamic world.

The klaxon of hurt Muslim feelings was also sounded by the Organization of the Islamic Conference (OIC) at the U.N. Human Rights Commission.

On March 31, 2011, Pakistan's United Nations ambassador, Abdullah Hussain Haroon, spoke to reporters at UN headquarters on behalf of the 56 member state Organization of the Islamic Conference (OIC) Ambassadorial Group, condemning the recent burning of a copy of the Koran by the pastors of a small Baptist Church in Gainesville, Florida. He highlighted the OIC's "grave concern that the despicable act had severely hurt the feelings of 1.5 billion Muslims around the world" and warned reporters that it could lead to "incidents that are uncontrollable."

Was that a "prophecy," a hope, or a threat?

The very next day Ambassador Haroon's warning turned into a tragic, self-fulfilling prophesy. A large mob of demonstrators in Afghanistan, angry at the Koran burning and apparently responding to calls for revenge by three mullahs who had addressed worshippers at Friday prayer in one of Afghanistan's holiest mosques, stormed a United Nations compound in the northern region of the country and killed a number of innocent people, including at least seven UN staff members - two reportedly by beheading.

Not to be outdone in condemning Jones for "causing" the Afghan riots, a number of American politicians, a Supreme Court justice, and one American general chimed in with their own "anger." South Carolina Republican Lindsey Graham, Senate majority leader Nevada Democrat Harry Reid, one Supreme Court justice, Steven Breyer, and General David H. Petraeus, commander of the NATO International Security Assistance Force (ISAF) and U.S. Forces Afghanistan, all piled on the hapless Jones.

Senate Majority Leader Harry Reid says congressional lawmakers are discussing taking some action in response to the Koran burnings of a Tennessee [sic] pastor that led to killings at the U.N. facility in Afghanistan and sparked protests across the Middle East, Politico reports. "Ten to 20 people have been killed," Reid said Sunday on CBS' "Face the Nation." "We'll take a look at this of course. As to whether we need hearings or not, I don't know."

Lindsey Graham was more specific, but just as ignorant.

> Senator Lindsey Graham said Congress might need to explore the need to limit some forms of freedom of speech, in light of Tennessee [sic] pastor Terry Jones' Quran burning, and how such actions result in enabling U.S. enemies. "I wish we could find a way to hold people accountable. Free speech is a great idea, but we're in a war," Graham told CBS' Bob Schieffer on "Face the Nation" Sunday.

ABC's George Stephanopoulos of "Good Morning America" reported these interesting instances of ignorance.

> We also saw Democrats and Republicans alike assume that Pastor Jones had a Constitutional right to burn those Korans. But Supreme Court Justice Stephen Breyer told me on "GMA" that he's not prepared to conclude that — in the internet age — the First Amendment condones Koran burning.

> Last week President Obama told me that Pastor Jones could be cited for public burning – but that was "the extent of the laws that we have available to us." Rep. John Boehner said on "GMA" that "just because you have a right to do something in America does not mean it is the right thing to do."

General Petraeus offered his own politically correct obloquy:

> "We condemn, in particular, the action of an individual in the United States who recently burned the Holy Quran. We also offer condolences to the families of all those injured and killed in violence which occurred in the wake of the burning of the Holy Quran.

> We further hope the Afghan people understand that the actions of a small number of individuals, who have been extremely disrespectful to the Holy Quran, are not representative of any of the countries of the international community who are in Afghanistan to help the Afghan people."

Where have all the great generals gone? Can you imagine George Patton being outraged over a desecration of *Mein Kampf,* or William Sherman frowning on a mocking rendition of "Dixie"?

Lastly, President Barack Obama consulted his script writer and had this to say:

The desecration of any holy text, including the Koran, is an act of extreme intolerance and bigotry. However, to attack and kill innocent people in response is outrageous, and an affront to human decency and dignity. No religion tolerates the slaughter and beheading of innocent people, and there is no justification for such a dishonorable and deplorable act.

Empty but ominous words. In Indonesia, as a boy, Obama reputedly studied the Koran, and should know better than any other politician that the Koran indeed tolerates – nay, encourages – the slaughter and beheading of non-Muslims and other infidels. Note that he specified the "text," and not the physical object. The "text" contains ideas that sanction a brutal ideology. Mr. Obama is certainly smarter than Terry Jones.

Daniel Greenfield of Sultan Knish, in his April 3rd article, "Muslims and Moral Handicaps," summed it up neatly on Sultan Knish. Citing the incident of a German propagandist jailed during WWI, he notes:

> Today we aren't jailing filmmakers who traffic in anti-American propaganda in wartime. If we did then half of Hollywood would be behind bars. Instead Democratic and Republican Senators are discussing banning speech offensive to the enemy. Because even though they're killing us already—we had better not provoke them or who knows how much worse it will become.

What it will all lead up to is a kind of selective censorship that will insulate Islam from any criticism. Politicians, generals and pundits do not become overwrought about the burning of bibles, Torahs, or other religious documents. Only about Korans. This is because Islam is always in the news, in some form or another, and that is because Muslims are always being "provoked" by the least criticism of them and their creed to throw bloody tantrums. Islam is another "culture," another religion, another "way of life," and by the criteria of political correctness and an affinity for dhimmitude, it must be protected from all forms of offense.

And that selective, privilege-granting censorship will serve as a precedent and lead to other brands of censorship, including prohibiting the kind of writing you are reading here. Calm, reasoned, and deserved criticism of Islam must sooner or later be classified as a "hate crime," as "injurious," "hurtful," and "bigoted" as burning a Koran. Observe the intellectual and moral stature of Americans who attempt to establish a causal relationship between the Afghan riots and Jones's publicity stunt-cum-protest.

These people are not going to defend the First Amendment. They are unable to. They are intellectual troglodytes. For evidence of the fishbowls of swirling, floating abstractions their minds are, I invite anyone to read the transcript of an interview of Lindsey Graham by The National Review and to reach his own conclusion ("Graham Responds to Steyn, Stuttaford:
The South Carolina senator defends his comments about Koran burning" April 4th). The interview was conducted to give Graham a chance to expand and qualify his weekend statements on the Afghan riots and Jones's Koran-burning. I challenge anyone to find an operating principle in his illiterate, emotionalist gibberish, the kind of equivocating rhetoric that can justify the kind of fascism that is congealing around American life. To wit:

> "Let me tell you, the First Amendment means nothing without people like General Petraeus. I don't believe that the First Amendment allows you to burn the flag or picket the funeral of a slain service member. I am going to continue to speak out and say that's wrong. The First Amendment does allow you to express yourself and burn a Koran. I'm sure that's the law, but I don't think it's a responsible use of our First Amendment right."

And if Graham, Boehner, Reid, Petraeus, and Obama do not think my writing here is a "responsible" use of my First Amendment right, what do they propose to do about it? How do they propose to make me "accountable"? The menacing growl is in their words. The First Amendment has already been whittled down to a splinter of what it once meant. It would be nothing to them to reduce it to a sliver.

What distinguishes their position on freedom of speech from that of the United Nations? Nothing. A U.N. spokesman felt compelled to add his own two cents about freedom of speech as he recounted the murders of the U.N. staff by the Muslim mob in Mazar-i-Sharif. Staffan de Mistura, the U.N's Envoy to Afghanistan, described the Koran-burning as an "insane and totally despicable gesture."

> "Freedom of speech does not mean freedom of offending culture, religion or traditions," de Mistura said. "Those who entered our building were actually furiously angry about the issue about the Quran. There was nothing political there."

Oh, but there was, Mr. Mistura. Freedom of speech now stands to be sacrificed on the altar of pragmatic accommodation to Muslims and Islam. And as a Graham or Reid or Boehner touch a match to a compromise-soaked Constitution, Muslims, gathering after their prayers, will watch the ashes and smoke rise in the sky, and chant: "Burn, baby! Burn!"

They will not need to chant, "Death to America!" America will already be dead.

April 2011

Cambridge University Adopts a Prayer Rug

In February this year, the general and guest editors of a Cambridge University newspaper, *Clareification*, were disciplined by the school's authorities for having published one of the Danish cartoons in a satire on religion, and were required to publish an apology to Muslim students.

Worse, the student/guest editor was "interviewed" by the local police for having putatively committed a "hate crime" (as defined under Section 5 of the Public Order Act), otherwise deemed, in hyperbolic British nomenclature, as an act of "harassment, alarm or distress." It was Muslim students who were said to be "harassed, alarmed and distressed" by the cartoon, not the general and guest editors. (*FrontPage Magazine,* April 18)

The apology was extorted from the student on pain of not only being expelled from Cambridge, but of possible arrest and imprisonment by the authorities for the alleged "crime." The student has had to go into hiding, *à la* Salman Rushdie.

If the student must go into hiding, isn't that an acknowledgement of – and concession to – the role of and sanction of physical force in the "belief system" by not only those who might want to kill or harm the victim, but by the university authorities and the British government? What would be required of the "harassed, alarmed, and distressed" Muslims to leave this individual's life untouched by their "anger"?

Asim Mumtaz, president of Cambridge's Ahmadiyya Muslim Association, said that he was "satisfied with the way the college [Clare College at Cambridge] had dealt with the situation." He said: "Religion teaches us that God is merciful and forgives, and we should forgive others as well, so long as this student realized the impact of their (sic) actions and that this was wrong. This student has a full life ahead of him and if he had been thrown out of the university that would have had a huge impact."

What are the implied alternatives in Mumtaz's statement? Assassination, Theo van Gogh style – unless the student "groveled" before his potential murderers with an apology, or a life on the run, or even imprisonment. What kind of "full life" has this student to look forward to now, or any student who dares speak his mind about Islam or any other creed? What "impact" will the cowardly resolution of this crisis have on this student's willingness in the future to exercise his freedom of speech or stand by his convictions?

Mercy and forgiveness are doled out only to the submissive – that's the Koranic way to let live or let die.

It is an error to think that the submission of Cambridge University to potential Muslim violence and its sanctification of alleged "hurt feelings" is a measure of Muslim power and influence. Evil by itself is impotent.

Instead, it is a measure of the abandonment of reason and objective values that gives the Muslims the appearance of power and influence to suppress freedom of speech. Any compromise between good and evil – or between reason and mysticism, or between the principle of freedom of speech and censorship – always will result in a victory for evil, mysticism, or censorship.

Ayn Rand made several crucial observations on the subject of compromise.

> "Contrary to the fanatical belief of its advocates, compromise [on basic principles] does not satisfy, but *dissatisfies* everybody; it does not lead to general fulfillment, but to general frustration; those who try to be all things to all men, end up by not being anything to anyone. And more: the partial victory of an unjust claim, encourages the claimant to try further; the partial defeat of a just claim, discourages and paralyzes the victim." ("The Cashing-In: The Student 'Rebellion'" – *Capitalism: The Unknown Ideal*, p. 255, 1966)

A principle by its nature is what it is, a recognized truth requiring consistent action. Failure to act on it when it conflicts with its antipode can only result, by default, in the establishment of the antipode as an ingredient of policy. If a principle, especially a rational one, is not defended and upheld in such a conflict, then it may as well not be recognized, and the appeasers and compromisers responsible for defending and upholding it must concede to that principle's enemies: "We are open to any pressure, to any threats of violence, to any brazen thuggery in the name of...." In this instance, it is in the name of "diversity."

Ostensibly, Cambridge acted from the "principle" of diversity, of trying to be all things to all men. In reality, it was a pragmatic, veiled capitulation to fear of the mob – more noisy Danish cartoon protests – that required the sacrifice of a lone individual to the mob's emotions.

"Diversity," as it is promulgated throughout Western culture, is the mantra of subjectivism, whim worshipping, and non-absolutes. In this instance, the violation of the policy of "diversity" can best be expressed from the Muslim standpoint: "You have mocked my icon, my particular ghost, and made him the subject of levity. My icon is sacred, and you must be punished. Never mind that he was a pedophilic, murderous, tyrannical bastard – the Koran and Hadith confirm these facts about him – Mohammed is my prophet and I will feel unworthy of his favor and of Allah's blessings unless I take umbrage to slanderous insults to or slurs on their persons."

"A Clare College spokesman said: 'Because of the gravity of the situation and the diversity of views expressed about the best way to handle it,'" the College settled for "'a course of restorative justice and reconciliation.'" Which meant the guest editor's apology and his mandated browbeating by "senior representatives of Cambridge's religious communities."

A noted outspoken foe of Islamism remarked: "Note that 'diversity of views' does NOT include the right to criticize Islam."

The Clare College statement said that a "note of apology was distributed to all college members. The college is now arranging a meeting for next term to discuss the problem of maintaining free speech while avoiding offence...."

The "problem" will prove to be insuperable. Freedom of speech and de facto censorship cannot be reconciled.

Rand stated three rules that govern the issue of compromise. Two of them are:

"In any *collaboration* between two men (or two groups) who hold *different* basic principles, it is the more evil or irrational one who wins"; and "When opposite basic principles are clearly and openly defined, it works to the advantage of the rational side; when they are *not* clearly defined, but are hidden or evaded, it works to the advantage of the irrational side." ("The Anatomy of Compromise," *Capitalism: The Unknown Ideal*, p. 145, 1966)

In the Cambridge instance, it is the Muslims – the irrational group – who have won (again). The Cambridge authorities could be accused of collaborating with the Muslims to abridge freedom of speech. And, because the concept of "diversity" is not clearly defined, but hides and evades – or abandons – the idea of freedom of speech, it worked to the advantage of the Muslim students.

This makes it possible for Muslims to consider "diversity" a one-way street, or a policy from which they demand, and are granted, exemption.

Under a headline not wholly coincidental with the Cambridge cave-in or submission to Islam, "Universities 'targeted' by Islamic extremists," the *Daily Telegraph* (London) on April 17 reported that Prof. Anthony Glees, of the Center for Intelligence and Security Studies at Brunel University in Britain, warned a conference of university security officers that Islamic "extremists" have targeted British universities as recruiting grounds for terrorists. "We must accept this problem is widespread and underestimated," said Glees. "Unless decisive action against campus extremism is taken, the security situation in the UK can only deteriorate."

> Cambridge is one of the universities Glees identified as infiltrated by an allegedly disbanded "extremist" group, al-Muhajiroun, in addition to Oxford, the London School of Economics, and the Imperial College. Prof. Glees stated that a rabble-rousing imam who preaches the Islamic conquest of Britain and death to infidels, and who was founder of al-Muhajiroun, contradicts the official government line that the group has been disbanded and claims it has a presence on several university campuses.

But, is it Islamic "extremism" that is widespread and underestimated, or is it the policy of "diversity" that poses the greatest danger, not only in Britain, but in the U.S., as well? Note the "extremism" which Cambridge took action against at the behest of its Muslim students: a student exercising his freedom of speech.

"Diversity" is an indiscriminate policy that treats as untouchable and exempt from criticism or rational scrutiny – and satirical cartoons are a form of criticism – any unsubstantiated belief or assertion. But since the nature of man requires rational, absolute evaluations and values in order for him to function and survive, a policy of "diversity" or of non-judgmental neutrality concerning those beliefs or assertions allows those with the most vocal assertions to fill the vacuum created by the abandonment of value judgments.

The Cambridge University authorities, like their diversity-bound, non-judgmental brethren elsewhere, refuse to condemn Islamic "radicalism" because it is too closely tied to Islam itself. Willingly or not, they must eschew any claim to neutrality and yield to the strongest, most vociferous pressure group.

A policy of "diversity" can only engender injustice, a pall of fear, and self-induced blindness. Ultimately, such a policy will impose the irrational by extortion or the point of a gun.

It would be unfair to single out a British university for adopting a prayer rug. When was the last time one heard of an American university or college newspaper offending Muslims? One could argue that fear-fueled political correctness and the prospect of official retribution for flouting it has moved Americans further along the path of moral decrepitude.

April 2007

Burning the First Amendment

In the classic western, *High Noon*, Will Kane, the retiring U.S. Marshall of Hadleyville, must face a gang of criminals who have come back to town, intent on vengeance on Kane for his having helped send the leader to prison. Most of the townspeople, in a demonstration of mass cowardice (a "terror-stricken town," as the trailer narrative goes), repair to a church after they have abandoned Kane, citing a host of rationalistic excuses. There they pray and squeeze their eyes shut in desperate hope that it is only Kane the gang will kill, and won't run amok in the town itself. But they would much, much prefer him to leave to save themselves the bother of having any moral backbone.

A deputy refuses to help out of personal jealousy, and resigns. A former mistress packs up and leaves. Even Kane's new wife, a pacifist Quaker, boards the train out of town, the same train that brings Frank Miller, the gang leader, into it. A young boy is the only person who volunteers to help Kane fight the gang.

The townspeople beg Kane to leave, more to protect their own hides than out of concern for his life. But for Kane, flight is not an option. He chooses to stay and face the gang because he knows they will eventually find him, wherever he goes.

Pastor Terry Jones of the Dove World Outreach Center in Gainesville, Florida, is not of the same mettle as Will Kane. Nor is Supreme Court Justice Stephen Breyer. Nor is President Barack Obama, nor is General David Petraeus. After promising to burn copies of the Koran in protest against the erection of the Ground Zero mosque (aka "community center") and against terrorism, Jones decided to not burn the Korans because he was warned that doing so might lead to Muslim rioting abroad and cause death and destruction.

Pastor Jones had a fundamental right to burn his Korans. They were his private property, or his church's. It was his or the church's money. His gesture was loony, not "counter-productive" as some pundits have claimed, but rather a futile protest against the Ground Zero mosque and Islamic terrorism. It may have even been a bid for publicity, which he certainly garnered.

What about burning Bibles, or copies of *Mein Kampf,* or *Das Kapital,* or even *Atlas Shrugged,* or the *Harry Patter* novels? The same principle applies. Freedom of speech is inherently linked to private property. If property is regulated, controlled, or abolished, then, by extension, so is speech. This is what Obama, Cass Sunstein, and the

FCC are creeping up to in wanting to regulate the Internet through "net neutrality."

However, the author of a Pajamas Media article on the Koran-burning and Justice Breyer's comments about it on "Good Morning, America,", does point to but does not raise a very relevant issue, which is the fear factor. Brow-beating or threatening Terry Jones (as is likely what happened) into canceling his over-publicized plan to burn some Korans — because burning them might provoke Muslims to riot and kill and run amok is (as they promised to do, and as they did), and possibly endanger our troops in Afghanistan and Americans in general — is, on the face of it, an act of submission to Islam.

President Barack Obama, technically, as commander-in-chief and representative of the American value of freedom of speech, should have filled Will Kane's shoes and defended Jones's right to burn the Korans. He should have taken a stand against the hue-and-cry of the press and Muslims and defended Jones' proposed action. But, in conformance with his "Muslim outreach" policy, he defended Muslim anger and not Jones.

> "This is a recruitment bonanza for al Qaeda," Obama said in an interview with ABC's "Good Morning America" program. "You could have serious violence in places like Pakistan or Afghanistan. This could increase the recruitment of individuals who would be willing to blow themselves up in American cities or European cities."

> "I just hope he understands that what he is proposing to do is completely contrary to our values as Americans, that this country has been built on the notions of religious freedom and religious tolerance," Obama said. "He says he's someone who is motivated by his faith ... I hope he listens to those better angels and understands that this is a destructive act that he's engaging in," Obama said.

Well, those "better angels" came down on Jones like a ton of bricks. General David Petraeus also wielded his cosh on Jones.

General David Petraeus said the planned torching of Islam's holy book by a Florida church would be a propaganda coupe for the Taliban in Afghanistan and stoke anti-US sentiment across the Muslim world.

> "It could endanger troops and it could endanger the overall effort in Afghanistan," said Petraeus of the plan. "It is

precisely the kind of action the Taliban uses and could cause significant problems. Not just here but everywhere in the world we are engaged with the Islamic community," the general said in an emailed statement.

Why should anyone care that the burning would have been a "propaganda coupe" for the Taliban or any other Islamic gang? And note that Petraeus said that we are "engaged with the Islamic community" — not *at war* with it. What is it that American lives and treasure have been spent on for the last nine years in Iraq and Afghanistan? Building "community centers"? And if so, aren't the troops in harm's way, with the Taliban and Al Quada and other Islamic gangs — all those "community leaders" — shooting at them already?

Defense Secretary Robert Gates called Jones to talk him out of the Koran-burning.

> U.S. Defense Secretary Robert Gates on Sept. 9 phoned a Florida pastor planning to burn Korans and warned him that he was putting the lives of U.S. soldiers at risk, the Pentagon said. Speaking to the pastor, Gates "expressed his grave concern that going forward with this Koran burning would put the lives of our forces at risk, especially in Iraq and Afghanistan, and urged him not to proceed with it," press secretary Geoff Morrell told reporters.

It is almost as though Obama, Petraeus, and Gates had watched *High Noon* and decided to adopt the cowardly pragmatism of not fighting the Miller-Muslim gang. "You'll only upset them and make them angrier than they already are. You'll just stoke the fires of hatred."

I have news for Gates: The hatred was always there, and the haters have never lacked an excuse to run amok. Imam Feisal Rauf also warned on the "Larry King Show" of a Muslim retaliation:

But, capping a day-long rhetorical offensive that began Wednesday morning with an opinion piece in The New York Times, Rauf said he intends to go ahead with the "multifaith" center near the site where Islamic terrorists killed nearly 2,800 people because not doing so would unleash fury abroad.

> "There is a certain anger here [in America], no doubt," he said later in the interview. "But if we don't do this right, anger will explode in the Muslim world. If we don't do things correctly, this crisis could become much bigger than the Danish cartoon

crisis [over images depicting the Prophet Mohammed], which resulted in attacks on Danish embassies in various parts of the Muslim world. And we have a much bigger footprint in the Muslim world."

"I am glad that Pastor Jones has decided not to burn any Korans," Rauf said in a statement read to ABC News' Christiane Amanpour.

Some "anger" is more equal than others. American anger over the Ground Zero mosque should be restrained and stifled, if not outright prohibited. Muslim "anger," however, is wholly justified and could "explode." How? Like car bombs? Shoe bombs? IED's? Fire-bombings? Homicidal rioting? Well, this is all out of the hands of the self-styled "bridge builder" and yearner for "peace and harmony."

Supreme Court Justice Stephen Breyer was interviewed by George Stephanopoulos on ABC's "Good Morning, America." Breyer, a liberal, hedged on the question of whether or not Terry Jones had a right to burn the Korans.

… Democrats and Republicans alike assume that Pastor Jones had a Constitutional right to burn those Korans. But Supreme Court Justice Stephen Breyer told me…that he's not prepared to conclude that — in the internet age — the First Amendment condones Koran burning. "Holmes said it doesn't mean you can shout 'fire' in a crowded theater," Breyer told me. "Well, what is it? Why? Because people will be trampled to death. And what is the crowded theater today? What is the being trampled to death?"

For Breyer, that right is not a foregone conclusion. "It will be answered over time in a series of cases which force people to think carefully. That's the virtue of cases," Breyer told me. "And not just cases. Cases produce briefs, briefs produce thought. Arguments are made. The judges sit back and think. And most importantly, when they decide, they have to write an opinion, and that opinion has to be based on reason. It isn't a fake."

Maybe, said the judge and mayor and townsfolk in the Hadleyville church to Will Kane, just maybe you're wrong. Maybe Frank Miller has a right to be angry with you. Maybe you hurt his feelings. You know that better than any of us. He's a bad man, but must have his good points, we don't know. Maybe he has a right to shoot you. We're not saying he should. We don't know. But, Will, you've got to look at this on a case by case issue. And it would be best if you just skedaddled, and saved us a lot of worry and grief. Who knows? Maybe we have a right to just hogtie you now and hand you over to Frank Miller ourselves (hah, hah) and save everyone a lot of trouble!

If one refrains from taking an action because the action may incur the wrath of Allah's followers or of Wontonka or Attila the Hun or the thug down the street, who is the winner? Imam Feisal Rauf, for example, has claimed that not allowing him to build his alleged "community center" near Ground Zero will be taken as an assault on Islam and provoke riots and vengeance and so on. But then none of these parties has a clue about the link between private property and freedom of speech, except, perhaps Obama, spiritual grandson of Saul Alinsky, enemy of private property and freedom of speech. Obama, Petraeus, Jones, and Breyer have all submitted to Islam.

This is how Sharia law is insinuating itself into political thought. We do not demand that Islam and Muslims defer to secular law and individual rights; we should concede that we should defer to Muslims and Islam, because it's a "religious freedom" issue, because if we don't, Muslims will be angry and begin flying planes into buildings again, and stabbing people to death, or shooting Americans at random, and causing all kinds of unpleasantness, when we really all we want is to get along with them and not be so judgmental, because that's such a bother.

None of these "moral leaders" had the courage and sense of consequence that Will Kane had. Collectively, they have told the Frank Miller gang (or Feisal Rauf) they can have the town.

Most other Americans, however, have demonstrated through the Tea Parties and their opposition to the Ground Zero mosque, that they still have the moral certitude of Will Kane. It is they who are telling looting politicians and dissimulating Islamic leaders to get out of town.

September 2010

Review for the Journal of Information Ethics

Burning Books and Leveling Libraries: Extremist Violence and Cultural Destruction, by Rebecca Knuth. Westport, CT, London: Præger, 2006. 233 pp.

One of the most sobering photographs from the London Blitz is of a bombed out library. Men in their fedoras, homburgs, and woolen winter coats stand in the rubble reading books that have survived the blast and fire. Ringing them are still-standing walls with scorched shelves of books, reaching almost to a roof that no longer exists. The books and the men are exposed to a gray, leaden sky. The men are engrossed in what they are reading, their faces tautly somber, almost oblivious to their circumstances, but perhaps conscious of the incalculable loss.

Rebecca Knuth's *Burning Books and Leveling Libraries* is also a sobering, tautly written account of how and why books and libraries have perished as a result of war, civil upheaval and totalitarianism.

The problem with Knuth's book is that it is basically written from a sociological premise, its power undercut by innervating and uneconomical sociological language. One cannot doubt Knuth's concern about the consequences of biblioclasm, that is, of book burning, the destruction of libraries and museums, and censorship by state policy or anarchic mob violence; she obviously feels very strongly about it. But the constant employment of sociological jargon throughout skews an otherwise thorough delving into the causes of "extremist" violence against knowledge and enfeebles her arguments against such destruction.

The *Oxford Dictionary* definition of *sociology* is, "The science or study of the origin, history, and constitution of human society; social science." The *Britannica Concise Encyclopedia* adds "interaction" and "collective behavior" to the definition. Sociology, in short, treats individuals as though they were mere reactive ciphers inhabiting a larger organism, "society"; it minimizes the role of volition and value choices. Its basic measure, as far as I can ascertain, is the statistic.

The chief culprit in this respect is the term "extremist," which occurs in the title and is used throughout Knuth's book. An "extremist" ideology or philosophy – as opposed to what? A "moderate" one? The sex act could be deemed an "extremist" manifestation of flirting. A favorite charge today is that reason needn't be taken to "extremes"; that it hasn't been accounts for the growing rule in the world of unreason, reason's "extremist" antipode.

The term "extremism" and its derivatives today are pejoratives for something complete, whole, or uncompromised, but nonetheless unwelcome, signifying that it is beyond a "norm." But, what is the norm of anything? No moral evaluation is ever expressed of extremism by Knuth, just a fearful disapproval.

Politically, for Knuth, the norm is *pluralism* (not to be confused with value-negating *multiculturalism*, but that is another issue), a term also frequently employed in her book. The *American Heritage Dictionary* defines it as "a condition of society in which numerous distinct ethnic, religious or cultural groups coexist within one nation." Pluralism is the abstract, "intellectual" expression of Rodney King's plaintive "Can't we all just get along?" How? By what rules or standards? How can these groups coexist without falling into civil strife if reason is neither respected by any of the groups nor enforced by authorities charged with maintaining the rule of law?

"Pluralism" is a secondary consequence, not a cause of civil society under the rule of law. It is reason and the rule of law that have, for example, permitted Baptists, Presbyterians, and atheists to live side by side in the U.S. without either group plotting another's decimation or persecution. These reflect the Enlightenment values that Knuth often cites as threatened or usurped by biblioclasm. However, the absence of reason, for example, underscores the failure of the U.S.'s attempt to create a "pluralistic" Iraq composed of Shiites, Sunnis, and Kurds, aged-old religious and ethnic enemies. Sociology offers no answers, and because it is a "value neutral" field of study – and I am no more inclined to call it a "science" than I am numerology – it can offer none. It can only observe and take notes.

Some terms and phrases repeatedly used in Knuth's book to account for the motives of those who burn books or firebomb libraries are "marginalized," "frustration," "social malaise," "unfulfilled needs," and "debilitating or alienating social circumstances." The instances are innumerable, but one should suffice to demonstrate how non-judgmental, value-neutral sociological language reduces what ought to be a moral issue to ashes. In Chapter 2, "Tracing the Path of Extremism from Robespierre to Milosevic," Knuth attempts to examine the motivation of individuals or groups that resort to violence against books and libraries in their own or other nations, and writes:

> "Distance and lack of purpose fed feelings of vulnerability and alienation. For the beleaguered, options perhaps seemed bleakly simple. They could (1) accommodate to the sweeping changes, no matter the price; (2) privately cling to traditional mindsets and risk having change sweep them to the wayside;

(3) fight back. (Bruce 2000, 117)" Later in that same paragraph, Knuth observes, "In what was essentially an 'escape from freedom' (Fromm 1941), vulnerable groups filled the vacuum of their existence with ideas that were comprehensive, compelling, and absolute." (p. 27)

What is conspicuously absent in the book is a moral judgment, a damning indictment. The language of sociology does not lend itself to such "extremism." The terms "killer," "murderer," "thug," and "criminal" apparently are not in the sociological lexicon. The most incriminating term Knuth uses in *Burning Books* is comparatively innocuous, "vandal."

Another term, not sociological, but used promiscuously throughout Knuth's book, is "democracy." Fundamentally, democracy is mob rule, employing legislated or direct force, of a majority or a politically empowered group over minorities or the public at large. One unintended irony of Knuth's book is that virtually every instance of book burning or library looting and destruction she cites with horrific, almost graphic effectiveness – by the Khmer Rouge, the Taliban, the Iraqis in Kuwait and later in Baghdad, the Maoists, or the Nazis – is democracy in action in its rawest or most "extreme" form.

Sociology does not examine, except in the shallowest, most superficial terms, the nature of man and his requirements for living. The concept of individual rights does not enter its worldview, only customs, traditions, beliefs, emotions, and subcultures. Sociology, by dispensing with moral appraisals of its subjects, such as "vandals" or criminal "extremists," implicitly exonerates them.

Knuth therefore shares the common, fuzzy notion (certainly not peculiar to sociologists by any means) that a democracy is the same thing as a political system that protects and guarantees individual rights – in this instance, the liberty to acquire knowledge without hindrance, fear, or risk of censorial penalty by mob or state. Democracy patently does not recognize or protect individual rights; it violates them on principle. The U.S. was founded as a rights-protecting republic; it has deteriorated into a group-warfare democracy. Look at Congress.

Later in her book, Knuth even permits herself to take a swipe at Allied policies during World War Two, when German and Japanese cities, together with their libraries and museums, were subjected to massive bombing. It is in these latter chapters that her pacifism surfaces and steers her thinking. It does not occur to her, in the course of bemoaning the "human and cultural losses" caused by the firebombing of Dresden and the atomic bombing of Hiroshima, that if Germany and Japan had won that war, or at least negotiated a "draw" with the Allies, the long-term consequences would have been harsher and more devastating.

Just as they are today, after the U.S. has for decades sanctioned and supported its committed enemies, particularly Islamic fundamentalism, which has been waging war against the West, in particular the U.S., for over thirty years. When Knuth addresses the subject of war itself, she is clearly out of her depth, and that subject is beyond the scope of this review. Her comments on the U.S.'s "militaristic" response to the attacks of 9/11 and her residual outrage, reserved for the U.S. for not preventing the looting of Iraqi museums and libraries by Iraqis after the fall of Baghdad, deserve a rebuke, not a review.

Discussing the sacking and subsequent destruction in 1933 by the Nazis of Berlin's Institute for Sexual Science, Knuth quotes Hitler in an off-the-record 1937 speech:

> "Today *we* claim leadership of the people, that is to say, we alone are entitled to lead the people as such – the individual man and woman. *We* determine the conditions under which the sexes live! *We* fashion the child!" (p. 115)

I was struck by how much that statement resonated in every particular with our own welfare state and especially the means and ends of American public education, which in large part are founded on a philosophy of sociology.

I had expected Knuth to dwell at length on the fundamental purpose of biblioclasm, whether practiced by mobs, religious crusaders, or totalitarians: to destroy evidence of the truth, and of the past, and to impose thought control. But, she does not. That would have entailed the application of a moral standard, an act forbidden to the children of modern American education.

January 2007

Wicked, Hurtful Words

Pat Condell, a retired British stand-up comedian and now an outspoken political commentator, regularly excoriates religions of all suasions on his own blog. In a recent video, he took Islam to the cleaners and, among other things, called Mohammed a desert nomad "with a psychological disorder" and said that women who wear the veil are "mentally ill." (See *The Dougout* blog, May 19.) He characterized average Muslims as "hysterical, murderous, carpet-chewing, book-burning Muppets." His atheistic humor may not be to everyone's taste – too often he is more outrageous than funny – but his monologues and observations have appealed to many of the non-faithful around the world. His *YouTube* videos have been broadcast just about everywhere. He reported that this particular video earned him 16,000 hits and a few death threats.

His latest monologue was sent to the Berkeley, California, city council. Members of that sorry enclave's "peace and justice commission" (more Marxist nomenclature you would need to conduct a search for) took grave exception to Condell's scathing critique of Islam and Muslims. "It's not about free speech," said Elliot Cohen, one of the commissioners. "It's hate speech." This commissioner also called it "racist."

Excuse me, Mr. Cohen, but, yes, it is about free speech. If we excluded what you deem "hate" speech from any protection, what would be left that you would permit to be spoken? Some vapid, meaningless, "balanced" exchange of views?

It is obvious that Condell's critique emanated from a hate for religion; in this instance, for Islam. And his contempt for adherents of that creed cannot be disputed. Conclusion: Condell "hates" Islam. So what?

However, Condell was not encouraging other atheists to go out and slay Muslims and torch mosques. He did not behave like American or British imams who advocate slaying infidels, torching churches and synagogues, and killing any Jews behind them; those genuinely "hateful" rantings are protected because they are founded on "religious" convictions. Condell's statements simply expressed an antipathy for Islam and were formatted in the vehicle of humor.

By some sleight of rationalization, however, it is asserted that Condell's statements should not be protected because they are not founded on any religious belief. Or, at least there are those who wish his statements were not protected by the First Amendment or the

British equivalent of it because they are fantasy-free, ergo, unexplainably immoral and wicked.

Watching Condell's video, I could not help but notice that as he ripped Islam to shreds, he did not sport a face-hiding balaclava or ski mask, the preferred headgear of those brave executioners and killers of Hamas and Hezbollah. Rather than looking like a wild-eyed, foaming-at-the-mouth crusader against the ghosts, phantoms and goblins of all faiths, he struck me a fiftyish, mild-mannered accountant or software engineer.

Cohen's "racist" charge against Condell is more serious. Given that Islam appeals to members of all kinds of races (remember Richard Reid, the foiled shoe-bomber?), black, white, Asian, Semite, non-Semite, this accusation makes no sense. To equate a serious or humorous critique of Islam with "racism" points to a very suspicious ulterior motive of the commissioner's, to wit, a desire to squelch all criticism of Islam. On the face of it, the "racism" charge is ludicrous. Condell has subjected Catholicism and Anglicism to the same treatment. Would the humorless commissioner call that criticism "racist," as well? On what grounds?

Condell was flaying a religion which is not so much a creed as it is an ideology. Ideologies, especially totalitarian ones, are as color blind as religions. Ask Castro, or Robert Mugabe, or Mao, or Stalin, or Hugo Chavez, or Vladimir Putin.

The Council on American-Islamic Relations and other Islamic organizations also equate criticism of Islam with racism, which is why they are so happy that the House of Representatives passed H.R. 1592, the Local Law Enforcement Hate Crime Prevention Act. It would make such "hate" speech a federal and punishable offense.

(On ABC News the other night, in special reporting on the recent death of Jerry Fallwell and the rise of religion in politics in the Reagan years, Charles Gibson noted that the Christian right is beginning to take up the cudgels on behalf of global warming, poverty, and AIDS. Well, there's intellectual bankruptcy for you.

In the same spirit of bankruptcy, the left is forming a kind of tacit, conditional alliance not only with Christians, but with Islamists, as well. Why would Cohen and Comrades care what anyone says about Islam, unless they saw something in it for them? It is reminiscent of the Nazi-Soviet non-aggression pact. They are all for imposing universal, collectivist power over the country as a shared goal. If they ever attain that goal, the falling out between them should be interesting, just as the Nazis and Soviets fell out, and be just as bloody.)

Further, what would Cohen propose to do about the likes of Condell and such "insulting, degenerating and racist" spewings? ("Degenerating"? Not "denigrating?" But, never mind, that's Cohen's vocabulary.) Advocate a government entity to police the Internet to keep it "clean" and "non-offensive"? And, why was Condell's video sent to Cohen and Comrades in the first place, and by whom? Was it sent to raise the good Marxists' hackles, to get them into a comical lather in the best Keystone Cops tradition? Or was it to provoke the bull with a red cape, to see if Cohen and Company could form a posse to lynch Condell from a distance of six thousand miles?

If the FBI or NSA confiscated Cohen's computer, they could track down the culprit, and determine his motive. I'm willing to bet the Internet cops would learn it was sent by the California chapter of either the Muslim Public Affairs Council or CAIR.

I am reluctant to let Condell monopolize "hate." Why is such speech called "hate speech"? What are the alternatives to that term? "Mildly resentful" speech? "Awfully irritated" speech? "A tad ticked off" speech? "Tepidly tactful" speech? The candidates are almost numberless. I will leave development of that kind of levity to Jerry Seinfeld, George Carlin, and Pat Condell.

I imagine that Cohen and Comrades could just as well seethe with anger at someone who exercised his freedom of speech by reciting in person or in a video, for example, the Declaration of Independence. Surely, Jefferson's language could be deemed "hate speech," directed against George the Third and Parliament, intended to move men to take action against those who shared the king's and his legislators' most profound beliefs. And, remember, they were all Anglicans, members of a state church, so the Declaration could be said to indirectly slur their religious beliefs, as well. Doubtless, George and many Englishmen found that language to be insulting, denigrating, and patently offensive. Also, radical. Perhaps, fearfully incomprehensible. Certainly hurtful.

After all, tyrants and dictators have feelings, too.

And everyone knows what happened as a result of that kind of speech: the violence of the American Revolution. Well, practically everyone would know whose minds haven't been turned to mush by a politically correct public school and college education.

Why have the advocates of censorship settled on the term "hate" to designate the kind of speech they disapprove of and wish to regulate? "Hate" is a powerful term, denoting an emotion rooted in fear. They presumably associate "hate" with action that is "likely" to be taken against that which is feared. Well, one can fear something without taking criminal action against it. Not everyone is an emotional, hate-saturated basket case like Cho, the student who gunned down 32 people at Virginia Tech. Most people will not act on their fears, which they usually cannot articulate except perhaps in the form of expletive-salted exclamations.

And what is it that the *gauleiters* of speech fear about "hate speech"? The truth. Ridicule of the indefensible. Disrespect for the fallacious. Not being taken seriously, after serious scrutiny or unmitigated hilarity has deflated their arguments. And communication by the offender of the truth, ridicule and disrespect to a wide audience whose members' minds are not controlled by the "offended."

For example, observe the peculiar outrage directed against anyone who questions the delusional fraud of man-caused global warming.

Speaking of hate speech, that globetrotting, church-going, odd couple, professional altruists and former presidents George H.W. Bush and Bill Clinton, addressed the graduating class of the University of New Hampshire last weekend.

> "…Putting politics aside Saturday," they urged " graduates to focus on helping others both in their communities and around the world….'I can't tell you the selfish pleasure I get out of working with President Clinton,'" said Bush. . (The *Daily Press*, Newport News, May 21)

Bush told an audience of 2,650 graduates "that they don't have to run for office to become leaders. 'All you have to do is care, roll up your sleeves and claim one of society's problems as your own.'" This is said in the state whose motto is "Live Free, or Die." The New Hampshire men who risked death at Bunker Hill to be free would slap Bush silly, if they could, for spewing such collectivist, anti-freedom claptrap.

If you ever doubted that the left and the right could ever meet in the middle to become an indistinguishable glob of collectivist politics, Bush Senior and Clinton will serve as a nonpareil symbol.

Adopt one of society's problems as one's own? Become a "caring," selfless minion of fascism, by obeying Kant's categorical imperative? Just like Elliot Cohen? And Jimmy Carter? And, don't forget Bill Gates, and anyone else who feels a guilt-driven compulsion to "give back" to society.

The double billing of Bush and Clinton in New Hampshire is an instance of a pair of idle, purposeless nonentities preaching altruism, and at taxpayer expense, as well. They both have Secret Service protection 24/7, at a cost of about $10,000 a day. The Secret Service goes with them even on their speaking engagements, from which these retired political millionaires each collect stupendous fees, in addition to their presidential retirement pay. One can only wonder how much the University of New Hampshire shelled out to them.

Unlike Voltaire, I won't defend someone's right to say things with which I disagree. I won't act to stop him, either, but try to answer him on my own dime and time. However, I bear a special malice for unrepentant frauds with careers of destruction who contribute to the diminution of my freedom, and I am forced to pay for it, as well.

There, dear readers, is another instance of "hate speech."

So, sue me.

May 2007

The Scarecrow of "Violent Language"

On the heels of excising the "hurtful" language from Mark Twain's novels, come the calls for mellowing the "caustic language" of anyone criticizing big government or its recent depredations against the country and its citizenry. The occasion is the attempted murder (the charge of "attempted assassination" is arguable; the victim was not a head of state) of Gabrielle Giffords, Democratic U.S. representative from Arizona, on January 8th during a political event outside a Safeway store in Tucson.

There is a drive on now to blame the Tea Party, "right-wingers," and any frank discussion of Obama and/or liberal politics for the shooting. The liberal/left is scrambling to cast a pall of "responsibility" on the authors of any "toxic rhetoric" alleged to have "encouraged" the shooter Jared Loughner to act out his fantasies and to "take action" against a perceived enemy. The abrupt shift of focus from Jared Loughner the mad man to the necessity of "civil" discourse could only be orchestrated by the left.

Philosophy 101: All of the blather has its roots in determinism. If one is constantly exposed to violence (or to "violent" words), one will be somehow programmed to commit violence, if not now, then at some time in the future. This idea views all men as ticking time-bombs who must be disarmed, even if it means removing their tongues. Ideally, they say, society should be an environment of fields of daisies and solar panels and unconditional tolerance for all, even for the insane. If one is constantly exposed to pacific rhetoric, one will always be disposed to peaceful demonstrations of agreement or opposition.

Determinism, of course, denies men their capacity for thought and volition. Whatever his mental state, whatever mental parallel universe his mind lived in, Loughner chose to do what he did. In reality.

It is almost laughable, watching the MSM, E.J. Dionne on the Washington Post, Paul Krugman in The New York Times, and others try to "pin the rap" on the Tea Party, conservatives, and anyone else deemed guilty by them of "hate speech" and "ugly rhetoric." It is so predictable. And, of course, on Sarah Palin (no, I am not a fan of hers). They are all "responsible" for the shooting. Poor Jared Loughner was just an unfortunate, receptive "pawn" of talk radio and indiscriminate "blogging." It is an "evil" environment that Loughner grew up in, so he cannot really be blamed for his actions. Only society. Or, rather, the "right" side of it. Up come the scarecrows of "violent" or "hateful" language.

Of course, The Council on American Islamic Relations (CAIR) is shedding crocodile tears over the event, when it has approved of far greater massacres in the name of Allah and has nothing to say about Hamas's goal of eliminating Israel, which would mean something greater than a shooting outside a grocery store. It is much like Al Capone or his lieutenant Frank Nitti sending flowers to the funeral of a rival gangster he has had rubbed out, complete with a nicely-worded card of consolation for the gangster's surviving family.

> In a statement, CAIR National Executive Director Nihad Awad said: "We offer sincere condolences to the friends, colleagues and family members of all those killed or injured in this brutal and senseless attack. We must come together as a nation to mourn the dead, pray for the speedy recovery of the injured and reject the extreme partisanship and inflammatory political rhetoric that can contribute to such tragedies."

We are not implying here that Giffords was a gangster. But, "inflammatory political rhetoric"? What was Loughner's "rhetoric," other than the diffuse, wildly careening statements of a deranged person that had no politically identifiable foundation, other than some inchoate conspiracy theory about government control of grammar and brainwashing, with a bias to the left? Conspiracy theories are a dime a dozen, with equal proportions shared by left and right. One truly could not fix one's "crosshairs" on what Loughner thought; the "target" keeps jumping around in and out of sight. Literally.

Michigan CAIR booster Dawud Walid wept copiously on his Weblog about the shooting, then played the Muslim victim card almost immediately.

> Now imagine if Loughner's last name was Muhammad, or if Loughner was a convert to Islam. Elected officials such as Rep. Peter King (R-NY) would be using yesterday's attack as further proof that American Muslims need to be watched closer and that we aren't doing enough to stop such attacks. And no doubt, media would be discussing now the looming danger of homegrown terrorism.

Just imagine it! Victimhood at last! Well, Mr. Walid, that was not what happened. But if there was ever a candidate for conversion to Islam, Loughner's application was exemplary and complete. He was growing more and more disconnected from reality and in need of a realm that would save him the effort of rational thought: Islam. Either that, or writing his ticket to a maximum security mental institution.

> I'd like for there to be more discussion in the media about the growing intolerance in America and the passive radicalization of America via the Tea Party Movement and their champion Sarah Palin regarding the caustic language environment that we live in which opens up the door to such attacks.

And if the "discussion" leads to the subject of Islamic violence around the globe, a violence sanctioned by vitriolic rhetoric by Islam's spokesmen, what will he have to say? No rebuttal is possible. If the "dialogue," "discourse," or "debate" does not go his way, and he loses the engagement, then what?

His wishes are being fulfilled. Islamists focus on "caustic language," namely any language that exposes Islam as a political/theocratic ideology bent on conquest and the establishment of universal Sharia law. The MSM and the liberal establishment are focusing on such language, as well.

The Washington Post published a rather insipid analysis of Loughner's "deteriorating mental state," and several readers took the bait to basically blame the First Amendment and Sarah Palin for Loughner's action. More interesting were those reader comments, which fell in line with the charge. Here, without correction of grammar or syntax, are some reader comments on The Washington Post article:

> "The nutcase was an avid Sara Palin fan. I hold Sara Palin and her rhetoric responsible for this mess."
> "People get killed and the gun nuts seem to rejoice in their peculiar interpretation of the 2nd amendment (which always seems to omit that "well-regulated militia" part). Very sad, predictable and unfortunately all too common in US culture."
> "The Palinisation of America is a sad thing to watch."
> "Yesterday, this forum was filled with the very hatred that Congressmen are saying caused the problem... as my congressman said it was rhetoric from the right that spurs such violence. The sheriff did his part by blaming political rhetoric as the cause. So all the name calling by people who are, I guess, still upset over the outcome of the elections. This was a crazed lunatic and the system let him go. A result of p. c. Innocent until he does something. Now we know more, and the sheriff should look at his comments and learn."

"Am I to believe that a mentally unstable young man watching newscasts of Tea Party attendees carrying guns to public meetings was not influenced by these images? Isn't that what he did? Listen to the anger of Tea Party defenders. Have these folks learned anything from this violent event?"

These comments echo Pima County Sheriff Clarence W. Dupnik's out-of-turn political remark about everyone being culpable for Loughner's mental state and the shooting, a remark which set the tone for what was to follow, a kneejerk smearing of anyone speaking his mind about the political state and direction of the country. Dupnik excoriated "the vitriolic rhetoric that we hear day in and day out from people in the radio business and some people in the TV business," and claimed that Arizona was becoming a "Mecca for prejudice and bigotry." (*That* will not sit well with CAIR or any other Islamic spokesman; it is tantamount to associating the Lourdes shrine with orgies, drug-dealing, and witchcraft.)

Dupnik later explained his remarks, saying they were made in "anger." So, who is guilty of making "vitriolic" statements? His explanation comes too late. His words framed the "debate," and words have consequences.

E.J. Dionne, Jr., the Post's pundit-in-chief, in a column, "Gabby Giffords, a tragic prophet," also did his part to paint the Loughner shooting in the darkest conservative and Tea Party colors. After extensively quoting Gifford on the political "language" that has characterized positions over the last two years, he goes on to point out:

> ... It is not partisan to observe that there are cycles to violent rhetoric in our politics. In the late 1960s, violent talk (and sometimes violence itself) was more common on the far left. But since President Obama's election, it is incontestable that significant parts of the American far right have adopted a language of revolutionary violence in the name of overthrowing "tyranny."
>
> It is Obama's opponents who carried guns to his speeches and cited Jefferson's line that the tree of liberty "must be refreshed from time to time with the blood of patriots and tyrants." It was Sharron Angle, the Republican candidate against Senate Majority Leader Harry Reid in Nevada, who spoke of "Second Amendment Remedies" And, yes, it was Palin who put those gun sights over the districts of the Democrats she was trying to defeat, including Giffords.

One imagines that Dionne's notion of perfect political discourse is for a president to endorse and sign socialist legislation and for citizens to just calmly say, "Gee, that's all wrong, it's violating my rights and this will bankrupt me, but we'll just go quietly and not make a fuss about it. Pardon us for interrupting." When a country is being "transformed" into a penal colony of servitude, are not its citizens permitted to express outrage and angry "rhetoric"? If they did not, they would deserve the incarceration.

Dionne concludes:

> Liberals were rightly pressed in the 1960s to condemn violence on the left. Now, conservative leaders must take on their fringe when it uses language that intimates threats of bloodshed. That means more than just highly general statements praising civility.

Translation: Anyone who cites the Constitution, quotes any one of the Founders about the proper role of government, or speaks passionately about the growing loss of freedom – even the freedom to speak one's mind – must be told to hush, or say it nicely, so as not to frighten anyone.

In short, this is an endorsement of *censorship*. No, wait. That is too *violent* an accusation. It might get freedom-of-speechers and First Amendment cultists "fired up" and we cannot predict what they will do, especially if they are also Second Amendment pistol-packers. Let us settle for the softer, more civil appellation of *public speech management*.

The New York Times dwelt on Loughner's "disjointed" statements (but, what is so enjoined about politicians when they profess a knowledge of economics and then saddle a country with trillion dollar debts?)

> He had posted on his MySpace page at some point a photograph of a United States history textbook, on top of which he had placed a handgun. He prepared a series of Internet videos filled with rambling statements on topics including the gold standard, mind control and SWAT teams. And he had started to act oddly during his classes at Pima Community College, causing unease among other students.

> The evidence and reports about Mr. Loughner's unusual conduct suggest an increasing alienation from society,

confusion, anger as well as foreboding that his life could soon come to an end.

Alienation? That one-size-fits-all excuse for becoming a homicidal maniac? Did the shooter alienate himself, or did "society" alienate him? One supposes that if Loughner were raised in an idyllic hugs-all-around-for-everyone society, he would have matured to discover the secret of gravity and patented the formula for a new kind of ambrosia.

Beating the Times is the paper's own prize ignoramus and alleged economist (caustic language intended), Paul Krugman. In his opinion piece, "Climate of Hate," he acts as a bellows to elevate the heat against freedom of speech. Not satisfied with "caustic language" or "hate speech," he invents his own term: "eliminationist rhetoric."

The point is that there's room in a democracy for people who ridicule and denounce those who disagree with them; there isn't any place for eliminationist rhetoric, for suggestions that those on the other side of a debate must be removed from that debate by whatever means necessary.

And it's the saturation of our political discourse — and especially our airwaves — with eliminationist rhetoric that lies behind the rising tide of violence.

Where's that toxic rhetoric coming from? Let's not make a false pretense of balance: it's coming, overwhelmingly, from the right. It's hard to imagine a Democratic member of Congress urging constituents to be "armed and dangerous" without being ostracized; but Representative Michele Bachmann, who did just that, is a rising star in the G.O.P.

Since long before Barack Obama was elected president, no Republican, no member of the Tea Party, no conservative, no libertarian, no Objectivist, no prominent "anti-government" activist has ever advocated assassination or even an armed rebellion against the federal government. The best of these individuals has simply reminded the administration and Congress of the proper role of government in as forceful *language* as possible – note that the term is forceful *language*, not forceful *action*. The focus has been on eliminating statist laws, not their authors. The day may come when action is justified, but that can happen only if the government moves to fit Americans with a velvet gag. When one is denied by force the power of words, the only alternative left to men to regain their freedom will be the power of force.

Krugman has already reached a conclusion about what ought to be done.

So will the Arizona massacre make our discourse less toxic? It's really up to G.O.P. leaders. Will they accept the reality of what's happening to America, and take a stand against eliminationist rhetoric? Or will they try to dismiss the massacre as the mere act of a deranged individual, and go on as before?

Yes, the massacre *was* the "mere act of a deranged individual" – the facts of reality are on the side of objective observers – and there is no reason to *not* "go on as before," possibly with the repeal of ObamaCare and other legislation favored by Krugman and his statist ilk across the country. While Krugman and his cohorts do not deny that Loughner was "deranged," they not so subtly imply that anyone who values his freedom and speaks without fear about his value of it is also "deranged" and a menace to society.

The government, the liberal/left in politics, and the intellectual establishment, are collectively guilty of their own "toxic rhetoric" – with the approving rhetoric of censorship.

January 2011

Fiat Theocracy: House Resolution 888

Too often bad news swirls into one's consciousness as abruptly as thousands of sparrows descending on an open field. Over the last week several newsworthy events occurred that demanded my attention, and at first it was difficult to decide which subject to address.

Should I dwell on Michael Chertoff, head of Homeland Security, who announced the need for national identification cards to combat illegal immigration and terrorism? The cards would be the capstone of a "security" system that is largely a sham and an outrageous and costly public relations ploy that dishonestly "assures" traveling Americans that their government is on the alert for terrorists. Giddy with the power of punishment he and his agency have over ordinary American citizens, who are presumed guilty until proven innocent by a privacy-violating frisk at airport checkpoints, he warned in the staccato tones of a drill sergeant at a news conference that residents of states that do not "cooperate" in the federal program would no longer be able to use their driver's licenses at airports as valid ID.

Why is Chertoff insisting now on creating a federal database to keep track of everyone? It is probably because he does not expect to be head of Homeland Security much longer, and wants to stick it to the country before a new president dismisses him.

Should I focus on Hillary Clinton, whose "teary moment" in New Hampshire last week was transparently calculated and orchestrated to win sympathy votes to jump-start her sputtering campaign for the White House, and who has just proposed a $70 billion federal "stimulus" package to rescue the housing market? Her political ambitions discount the fact that Federal "stimulus" packages of any nature are about as life saving for the economy as an injection of diluted arsenic is for a stroke victim. This is aside from her obsession with imprisoning everyone in a national health care plan, which would cost many more billions, and which maybe, just maybe, might be as efficient and efficacious as that of Great Britain, Canada, and of other semi-socialist countries.

Daniel Pipes, in his January 10 *Jerusalem Post* review of a new book that corrects the standard political spectrum and puts fascism where it actually belongs, as a necessary and inevitable partner or socialism, *Liberal Fascism: The Secret History of the American Left from Mussolini to the Politics of Meaning*, by Jonah Goldberg, cites the author's chronology of that secret history.

It begins with Woodrow Wilson's Progressivism policies (which gave us the Federal Reserve system and the income tax) and ends with

Clinton hoping "to insert the state deep into family life," which Pipes correctly interprets as an essential step of totalitarianism. State involvement in family or personal life was standard policy in Nazi Germany, Fascist Italy, Imperialist Japan, and Soviet Russia. It is still so in Communist China and all Muslim countries.

Pipes writes of Goldberg's book:

> "To sum up a near-century of history, if the American political system traditionally encouraged the pursuit of happiness, 'more and more of us want to stop chasing it and have it delivered.'"

True enough. Or do I then fault Pipes for his interpretation of "conservatism"? He writes in the same review that in contrast to fascism, "conservatism calls for limited government, individualism, democratic debate, and capitalism. Its appeal is liberty and leaving citizens alone." Perhaps that characterization of conservatism might have been accurate over a century ago. The "conservatism" practiced by Republicans in Congress, however, has been, ever since Wilson's time, more or less in partnership with progressivism's social legislation, which has never been seriously challenged either in Congress or by the Supreme Court.

Looking around at our culture, where can one find that "limited government," or the "liberty," or the government "leaving citizens alone"? Republican conservatives are as much to blame for the creeping totalitarian socialism in our lives as are the Democrats. They have consistently refused to discard the altruist element in their political philosophy, and consequently can only second any proposals to fit the nation into the straightjacket of statism. One must ask: What is it that "conservatives" wish to "conserve," if not the status quo, which, ever since at least Teddy Roosevelt's administration, has been anything but?

And while Pipes is perceptive enough to appreciate Goldberg's thesis, his perspicuity does not extend to distinguishing between "democracy," which is mob rule (debates or not), and the principles of individual rights, which our now much-emasculated *republican* form of government was supposed to protect against the populist assaults of *democracy* without any debate on the matter.

(But then, Pipes, a leading authority on the Islamic jihad against the West, unfortunately believes that our salvation lies in "moderate" or "reformed" Islam, which is much like believing that Andy Hardy could single-handedly repel a Nazi Tiger tank offensive during the Battle of the Bulge.)

I swore to myself that I had finished discussing God and religion, but something perilous has come to my attention: a subtle but sleazy attempt to make Christianity the official state religion of this country.

One of the most enduring but pernicious myths about the United States is that it was founded as a specifically and exclusively Christian nation. The fallacy is not the monopoly of evangelicals, or of politicians such as Mike Huckabee, Mitt Romney, or Barack Obama. It is an unquestioned and undigested fallacy that is simply passed on to the average American without any thought, qualification or insight, much as was the assertion of divine right of kings to rule in Europe, most of whom presumed to act as "God's stewards" (now it is unelected European Union bureaucrats).

Few politicians and establishment pundits challenge the fallacy, or dare to. It ignores the fact that when America declared its independence from Britain, it was solely on the grounds of political freedom, whose philosophical, intellectual roots were fundamentally secular in nature. That political freedom was established in the real world, and had nothing to do with God.

If God was mentioned at all in the course of the country's founding, it was a God that the founders understood did not interfere in human affairs and played no part in their political endeavors. Many of the founders were tactfully agnostic or were discreet atheists. The concept of God and the morality of altruism, which is the basis of Christian faith, to the most intellectually active of them, such as John Adams and Thomas Jefferson, were not compelling issues, neither to refute nor to impose as dogma on the American people. Religion was a private matter.

House of Representatives Resolution 888, sponsored by Virginia conservative Republican J. Randy Forbes (Chesapeake) is in effect an attempt to repudiate the Enlightenment and the secular political principles championed by the Founders and incorporated into the country's original political documents. It is an endorsement of medieval morality and intends a *de facto* establishment of one of the things that the Founders feared and fought a war to prevent from coming about: a state church or state religion.

> The resolution, cosponsored by thirty-one other representatives, including two others from Virginia, was referred to the Committee on Oversight and Government Reform on December 18, 2007. Its preamble reads:
>
> *"Affirming the rich spiritual and religious history of our Nation's founding and subsequent history and expressing*

> *support for designation of the first week in May as "American*
> *Religious History Week" for the appreciation of and education*
> *on America's history of religious faith."*

One would need to be a fulltime scholar with a hefty advance from a publisher or a foundation grant to take the time to answer each historical "whereas" in the resolution. Each of the seventy-four conjunctions requires setting a context, which the resolution glibly neglects to do.

The conjunctions comprise a tossed salad of citations of historical events, such as inaugural ceremonies, of engravings or images on public buildings, or of quotations from some of the Founders, past presidents, and Supreme Court opinions about God and the Christian faith, God's presence in mottos and coinage, and so on, which are all somehow supposed to add up to: a Christian nation!

A few of the more ludicrous ones should be mentioned here. Number sixty-six points to "the top of the walls in the House Chamber," on which "appear images of 23 great lawgivers…but Moses (the lawgiver, who – according to the Bible – originally received the law from God,) is the only lawgiver honored with a full face view, looking down on the proceedings of the House." Doubtless looking down with approval, as that Chamber betrays, sells out, and whittles away American freedoms.

Number seventy-two states that "in the Library of Congress, The Giant Bible of Mainz, and The Gutenberg Bible are on prominent permanent display and etched on the walls are Bible verses…." Well, I have a Bible in my reference library, together with some prayer books. The presence of these in my home do not make me a Christian, anymore than my owning a copy of *Das Kapital* or *Mein Kampf* makes me a communist or a Nazi.

Number three claims that "political scientists have documented that the most frequently-cited source in the political period known as The Founding Era was the Bible." Not true. The most frequently cited sources in that period by political theorists and philosophers were ancient Greek and Roman political tracts, together with Enlightenment political thinkers.

Number seven cites the Declaration of Independence and its four references to God. Of course, Forbes and his cosponsors would never explain that the chief reason for that is that British political philosopher John Locke, in whose language the Declaration was written, ascribed political rights in men to the work of a "retiring" God. He was wrong about that one thing, and right about just about everything else. But, that was the spirit of the times. Men were focused on elucidating the ideal conditions for living on earth, not on refuting a hand-me-down mythology with its promise of an afterlife.

Perhaps the most offensive in its implication to me was Number twenty-eight, which states that "…in 1853 the United States Senate declared that the Founding Fathers 'had no fear or jealousy of religion itself, nor did they wish to see us an irreligious people…they did not intend to spread over all the public authorities and the whole public action of the nation the dead and revolting spectacle of atheistical apathy.'" Anyone who has read my commentaries here knows that I am neither dead, nor revolting, nor apathetic.

Forbes's resolution has met with voluble opposition. According to a *Daily Press* (Newport News, VA) article of January 13, "Forbes seeks official nod to religion,"

> "…[C]ritics – ranging from atheists and Wiccans to mainstream civil rights groups – have accused Forbes of offering a distorted historical record and trying to use government authority where it isn't needed."

> "'We don't need the government to tell us that religion is important,' said Jeremy Gunn, director of the American Civil Liberties Union's program on freedom of religion and belief."

> "'I don't think Congress should embrace false history,' said Barry Lynn, executive director of Americans United for Separation of Church and State."

Gunn and Lynn are missing the point on two counts. Forbes's resolution is intended to establish religion as official federal policy – what else could it be if it were approved by an elective body? And "false history" – or fabricated "facts" or contextless assertions about facts (see "Hoary Old Chestnuts")—never checked or overruled a religionist's emotional fervor.

Forbes, smarting from criticisms he obviously did not expect, according to the *Daily Press* article, countered, "The essence of what they believe is that God is a myth. Why is it that these people become so venomous when you talk about God?"

They wouldn't, if he refrained from trying to force religion and that myth down their throats, and in the bargain make such critics political outcasts. "No legitimate person can say faith and religion haven't played an enormous role in the history of this country," said Forbes. *Legitimate* persons? Is he implying that a person who did not believe in God or acknowledged the over-emphasized role of religion in American history or who objected to rewritten history is *illegitimate*? That is, a non-person in the spirit of Michael Chertoff's national ID standard? And the venom is in his imagination, to judge by the few calmly worded criticisms that were reported in the press.

One of the Founders' objections to the British Crown's policies was the plan to establish in the colonies an episcopate or bishopric of the state Church of England, which, as it did in Great Britain, would have had all authority over religious matters, and have been supported by taxes levied directly on the colonists, regardless of their religion. The state church in America, as it did in Britain, would have "tolerated" faiths other than the Anglican, but not permitted them their own churches – only chapels – and have probably required, as it did in Britain, that all political and military offices be filled with men who were of the Anglican faith and who took the "test oath," subscribing to the rites and articles of the Anglican Church. The political implications of "packing the court" with Crown appointees, judges, legislators and functionaries all amenable to all oppressive Crown policies, should be obvious.

It was obvious to the Founders, and also to many American, non-conformist, non-Anglican ministers, most of whose Sunday sermons throughout the pre-Revolutionary period up to the Declaration of Independence were actually political disquisitions against the Crown and eloquent appeals for political liberty. In lieu of a 100,000-word book on the political stance of these clerics in answer to the allegations in Forbes's resolution, I offer a few excerpts from their sermons, which can be found in Franklin P. Cole's *They Preached Liberty*, a collection of statements by New England ministers, chiefly of Massachusetts, published by Liberty Press in Indianapolis.

"Those nations which are now groaning under the iron scepter of tyranny were once free; so they might probably have remained, by a seasonable precaution against despotic measures. Civil tyranny is usually small in its beginning, like 'the drop of a bucket,' till at length like a mighty torrent or the raging waves of the sea, it bears down all before it, and deluges whole countries and empires. Thus it is as to ecclesiastical tyranny also – the most cruel, intolerable, and impious of any…." Jonathan Mayhew of Boston, 1750.

> "Arrogant pretenses to infallibility in matters of state and religion, represent human nature in the most contemptible light." Samuel Cooke of Cambridge, 1770.

"The great and wise Author of our being has so formed us that the love of liberty is natural." John Tucker of Newbury, 1771.

"Our danger is not visionary, but real. Our contention is not about trifles, but about liberty and property." Gad Hitchcock of Pembroke, 1774.

"The God of nature has taught us by the situation and uncommon advantages of this place, that it was designed for extensive business: and here our fathers planted themselves, that they and their posterity might prosecute those branches of trade and merchandise which give riches and strength to nations and states." John Lathrop of Boston, 1774.

"No man denies but that *originally* all were equally free. Men did not purchase their freedom, nor was it the grant of kings, nor from charter, covenant, or compact, nor in any proper sense from man: But from God. They were born free." Samuel Webster of Salisbury, 1777.

The focus, as one can see in these examples and in numerous quotations throughout *They Preached Liberty*, was on political liberty, not on God. If a God existed, these men were of the position that he left it to men to achieve their freedom and happiness on earth. Observable nature, they thought, commanded men to contrive the best way to live with one another, not an unobservable supreme being. Their political thinking was as distant from the crude, barbaric dictates of the Ten Commandments as Pluto is from the Sun.

Representative Forbes, however, wishes to fabricate American history in the spirit of the Bible, which itself was woven from whole cloth. To paraphrase Jonathan Mayhew, perhaps the most "worldly" and consistent of the Massachusetts ministers, Forbes's resolution is a "drop of the bucket" which, if not opposed by Americans, might portend the establishment of ecclesiastical tyranny.

January 2008

Culture

Liberty, or The Lawn Chair

What a difference sixty-five years makes – in the culture. When Warner Brothers released *Casablanca* near the end of 1942, America had been at war for a year. Everyone knew we were at war, and knew also that complete victory over Nazi Germany and Imperial Japan was an absolute necessity. *Casablanca* echoed that knowledge.

There was no thought of compromise, of negotiating a "peace," or of "reaching out" to the American Nazi Bund for its help in reaching a trilateral rapprochement with Germany, Japan and Italy. There was not an ounce of angst over collateral casualties among the enemy population. When the U.S recovered from being attacked at Pearl Harbor, it eventually took the war to the enemy, and when it was victorious, and while the enemy's citizens struggled to survive amid the rubble and ashes of their folly, the U.S proceeded to root out that enemy's ideology of tyranny and conquest.

The U.S. is at war again. The culture, however, has not produced anything like *Casablanca*. (An exception is *300*, an allegory on the war, which our enemies immediately protested as "insulting.") It will not, cannot. The dramatization of moral values remains in the hands of Hollywood's nihilists and subjectivists. What we get instead are insipid comedies, computer animated cartoons, the occasional "war" movie that denigrates our military, and a steady parade of forgettable movies. This is because while the U.S. rooted out the enemy's ideology over half a century ago, it failed to eradicate the underlying philosophy that drove that ideology.

A philosophy that remains uneradicated, or is left submerged but intact, will resurrect itself, and take unexpected forms of expression. This

129

is true of a rational philosophy as well of an irrational one. With the collapse of the Roman Empire, reason all but vanished from men's lives as a norm. It began to rise again a thousand years later during the Renaissance. In the ensuing Enlightenment it gradually displaced faith and other forms of irrationality as a philosophical guide for living on earth.

But not entirely. Irrationality in its many forms remained on the periphery of especially 19th century Western culture and its political and intellectual life. It received a boost of energy to re-insinuate itself into men's thinking and lives and policies because reason had no consistent advocates and defenders. The irrational gained more and more ground in Western culture in the 20th century and has certainly infected the 21st.

It has reached its ultimate absurdity: we are at war with Islamism – a political/theological ideology that seeks to either destroy or conquer the West, its proponents have made that abundantly clear – but the West's political and moral energies are focused on irrelevancies elevated to global and domestic crises: AIDS, world hunger and poverty, global warming, the absence of universal health care, and so on.

One might think that our political leaders are in denial about the peril of Islamism, or Islamofascism, or Islamic imperialism. But denial is a conscious action – a refusal to acknowledge the reality of a thing. No, they are oblivious or indifferent to the peril. They are obsessed with other fish to fry other than our enemies. They wish to compel men to submit, not to Allah, but to their own brands of collectivism and tyranny.

Our leaders are paragons of compromise, they wring their hands over real, imagined or projected collateral casualties among the enemy's population, and have no qualms about "reaching out" to organizations such as the Muslim Brotherhood and Fatah to attain some kind of rapprochement with the enemies of the West – Iran, Saudi Arabia, Syria, North Korea, to name but the larger enemies – in the pursuit of the Kantian ideal of "peace" for its own sake. 9/11 has not been forgotten by our leadership; it has been demoted to irrelevancy.

The irrationalism of President George W. Bush – his refusal to acknowledge the existence and nature of our enemies, because altruism has corrupted his grasp of reality – has played no little role in the creation of the absurdity. His political enemies in this country probably feel grateful that he has made a mess of the war; he has given them an excuse to demote it and abandon it.

But his enemies are also corrupted by altruism. It is through altruism that they wish to acquire and impose freedom-destroying power. Lord Acton identified that fact, and the fact will not go away.

What inspired this commentary was the release last week of the American Film Institute's list of the 100 "greatest" American films, which is apparently compiled every ten years. *Casablanca* was number 3 on the list, *Citizen Kane* number 1, and *The Godfather* number 2. I could not help but note the significance of *Casablanca*'s ranking, which dropped from second place in 1998 to third this year. According to the *Daily Telegraph* (London) article on the list of June 22, the list "is determined by a jury of 1,500 filmmakers, critics and movie historians."

Of course, a vote of hands cannot establish the greatness of anything, least of all the esthetic value of art. Greatness is something that can only be recognized and established by individual minds, not by consensus. But, one can deduce from the rankings of 100 "greatest" American films that some positive esthetic measurement remained in some of the balloters.

I won't attempt here to second-guess the motives of the AFI balloters. *Casablanca* could have been appreciated by a large block of voters who valued its story and style. It is not the greatest American film, but it has an integrity to it that is effective and memorable. It is a war film, but the thing most absent in it is the war. *The Godfather* is virtually unparalleled in depicting the gradual corruption of an otherwise decent man. "It's not me, Kay," Michael Corleone tells his fiancé early in the film, when she wonders if many of the men at the wedding party are really gangsters. "It's my family."

In the end, however, it *was* him; he had no argument against the family-tribal loyalty that passed as a moral code among the gangsters and which demanded his action. By the end of *Godfather II* (number 32 on the AFI list), he has betrayed or destroyed everything that ever mattered to him. In the poignant last scene of the sequel, he sits alone in a lawn chair, a shell of his former self, contemplating the desolation of his life, yet still in denial of the fact that he was in any way responsible for it.

Rick Blaine, the night club/casino owner in *Casablanca*, by the end of the story rediscovers the values he thought he had lost, a blow that had turned him into a pragmatic cynic who tolerated the corruption around him. It is in his power to destroy them – Ilsa, his former romantic interest, and Victor Laszlo, the Czech patriot on the run from the Nazis – but his old character reasserts itself and he acts to preserve them. He gives the couple the transit papers to freedom.

About *Casablanca*, Ralph J. Gleason wrote in 1973, "those were times where things were so much simpler; the good guys and the bad guys were so much more clearly defined and the struggle itself, the moral imperative for man, so much more easily seen." (From the Introductory Note in *Casablanca: Script and Legend*, The Overlook Press, 1973.) That "imperative," writes Gleason, "is rarer now and in the whole visible world has a kind of institutionalized concrete dimness."

But, it was not a moral *imperative* that in the end moved Rick Blaine to action. It was a moral *choice*.

Americans, betrayed by their political and intellectual leadership over the current war (and over the decades), face the choice of becoming a Rick or a Michael Corleone. They can rediscover what it is to be an American, or they can surrender that identity and blame the world for their misery and just drift towards tragedy and an ignominious end. They can redeem themselves, or resign themselves to a logical and merciless fate.

The choice is clear: liberty, or the lawn chair.

(This article appeared on Rule of Reason as "Rick vs. *The Godfather*.")

June 2007

Review and Interview: *The Camp of the Saints*

Roland Shirk, contributor to Robert Spencer's *Jihad Watch*, on December 13th recommended a novel to the site's readers, Jean Raspail's
The Camp of the Saints, published in France in 1973 and in translation in the U.S. in 1975.* Shirk suggested it, with reservations, because it predicted and dramatized what would happen to Europe, particularly to France, if it allowed the mass immigration – actually, an invasion – of a million impoverished Hindus, first into France, and then into the rest of Europe: the downfall of Western civilization. The relevancy was the mass immigration of Muslims, which, at the time of publication of Raspail's novel, was a non-issue. Now the parallels are apparent to all but those whose minds have been lobotomized, suborned, or silenced by political correctness and various other liberal/left maladies.

Jean Raspail is the author of a few dozen books – travels, novels, nonfiction – and in 1981 was awarded the Grand Prix du Roman by the Académie Française.

Shirk introduced his recommendation of the novel with a likening of the mass immigration and the dissolution of French culture by Third World hordes to 9/11 and the planned erection of an Islamic victory monument at Ground Zero, Imam Feisal Rauf's mega-mosque. It would replace a building damaged by the attack on the World Trade Center, paid for with American taxpayer money and laundered funding likely Saudi in origin, with smaller contributions from Persian Gulf fiefdoms.

Shirk's principal reservation is here:

> Yes, race is used too overtly as a metaphor for the values of the West in *The Camp of the Saints*. At times, you can't help cringing at how concretely the author equates whiteness with Westernness. That overly material, almost biologistic racialism, if it were more than a metaphor, would be morally reprehensible. But the author is careful at various points to point in another direction: Most of his white characters are cringing, puling post-Christian slave moralizers who seem to deserve their onrushing fate; some of his most heroic, civilized figures are Indians who cherished their Western educations, who wish to help save the West.

Family Security Matters (FSM) interviewed me about *The Camp of the Saints*.

FSM: What prompted you to read *The Camp of the Saints*, aside from Mr. Shirk's recommendation?

Me: I hadn't read it in decades, and remembered little about it. What piqued my interest was the nature of Shirk's comments about it and his reservations about Raspail's "biologistic racialism" and how he went about defending Western values and liberties. He referred to the abrupt invasion of France by what he called "by hordes of culturally and religiously alien interlopers," with no conditions of assimilation imposed on them as the beginning of the end
of Western civilization.

FSM: Were his reservations justified?

Me: Oh, yes, very much so. But first let me get one issue out of the way. I haven't read any of Raspail's other books, and don't plan to, but, literarily speaking, *Camp* is an awful novel, a mess beyond redemption. There is little or no plot, all of the characters are two-dimensional, and pages and pages of it are either expository or just talking heads. I don't think it is the fault of the translator, and there have been two English translations of the work. Allen Drury, for example, was much better at writing that kind of doomsday-geared story, about the consequences of contemporary political machinations, domestic and international. Many of Raspail's historical references are obscure, or not well integrated into his central premise. As satire, or even as a serious parable, it's not very funny, and much of the intended humor is over my head.

Another drawback to the novel is Raspail's apparent distaste for paragraph breaks. A single paragraph of his can go on for pages, Kantian-style. Such long paragraphs are a mark of bad writing, of not knowing where to stop or pause to allow a reader to digest anything but in a humongous lump. It's a sign that the writer's ideas are an undifferentiated, unintegrated mass of floating concepts and ideas.
Ironically, given the cataclysmic nature of the subject, there is almost no drama in his narrative or dialogue.

Reading the novel was like watching a pot that never boiled, or waiting for a glacier to nudge a stone in its relentless push forward. Some of it is darkly but unintentionally comic, such as when a group of monks and Catholic officials in ecclesiastical garb attempt to "ward off" the disembarking hordes of Hindus on the French coast by just "being there," holding up a monstrance containing the Eucharist, as though it were a wreath of garlic and the hordes were vampires. They're either trampled to pulp by the barbarians, who don't even notice them, or they're swept up in the onrush of the barbarians as they move forward to claim the landscape and are never seen again. Raspail may have intended a point to that scene – he was very critical of the Church for allowing faith to lapse into mere empty-worded ritual – but it wasn't well delivered. Oh, he made many points, but it was agony getting to them.

FSM: You say Raspail was critical of Christianity, or the Church. Did he discuss the Hindu religion?

Me: Not once. They were born Hindus, their religion and culture were in their genes. He also ascribed Western values as practically genetic in nature for whites. As he presented the conflict between the West and the Hindus, it boiled down to a clash of gestalts, or collectives whose members couldn't help being what they were. The Western gestalt is superior to the Hindu, because….well, Raspail claims it is but never really offers a reason why. He couldn't without ascribing superiority and inferiority to race.

FSM: How?

Me: Raspail flays the whole Western apologetic, guilt-driven, self-loathing philosophy that he holds responsible for the invasion of the barbarians. When Belgium announces that it is adopting no more Hindu babies to be settled in Belgium, it precipitates the decision to sail to the West from Calcutta clear to France. That may have been his pronouncement on the repercussions of unconditional and limitless Western foreign aid to the Third World. The Third World became addicted to it, eventually claiming the aid as an entitlement. When it was withdrawn, somehow this gestalt of upset Indians decides to sail West to claim it, and, as an act of vengeance, settle there.

The difference between why the Hindus invaded Europe in the novel and why the Muslims have invaded it is crucial to note. The Hindus just wanted to settle in "paradise" and no mention is made of imposing an ideology on non-Hindus. The Hindus depicted by Raspail are actual brutes whose minds couldn't conceive of an ideology. No mention is made of their converting churches into Hindu temples, although they do proceed to trash the country and subjugate the white French citizens, many of whom decide to become "token blacks," or, as Raspail calls them, "fellow travelers."

In reality, Muslims were invited to settle in Europe to shore up its various welfare states, to do all the menial work that Europeans didn't wish to do or thought was beneath them. Raspail mentions Arabs and blacks from various other Third World venues preparing to take over Paris and other French cities once the million Hindus have made landfall in southern France.

I will remark that I found reading the novel so depressing that I had to take a break from it and often take two mental medications as antidotes to the doomsaying. One was the finale of Antonio Salieri's *Axur, re d'Ormus*, the other was the finale of Mozart's *Abduction from the Seraglio*. These are products of Western culture (among many, many more in the arts) which the nihilist intelligentsias have deprecated and which the Islamists wish to erase from man's memory and kill his capacity to produce and enjoy.

The only truly dramatic event in the story occurs early on when a retired professor of literature, observing from his villa on the Cote d'Azur the refugee fleet sitting offshore, has a brief discussion with a hippie nihilist character. He then shoots the foul-mouthed creature because he hoped that the Hindus would destroy everything the professor held dear. This malevolent, nihilist hippie, however, was right in his prediction of what would happen. His ilk in the elitist intellectual class, the professor recognizes, were responsible for the feeble, appeasing policy the government eventually adopts when confronted with a mass invasion of the "needy."

It was the nihilist intelligentsia who convinced the traditionalists that they had no case and no justification to deny the uncouth and unschooled hordes from India their right to the products of Western culture and their right to smother the West with their numbers. And the traditionalists folded. The nihilists and the traditionalists get their just desserts at the hands of the hordes: they're slaughtered, their wives and daughters taken into concubinage or sent to Hindu-only brothels, their homes and wealth taken over by Third World looters, squatters, and educated Third World racketeers.

This is exactly what has happened vis-à-vis Muslims and their campaign to take over Western countries. Underlying Islamic supremacism is a hatred for the life-affirming superiority of Western civilization. In this hatred Muslims share with the nihilists a malevolent approach to anything free – free men, free minds.
Raspail cites the racism of the Hindus, Muslims, and blacks and paints some very gory pictures of their reign over whites. These are echoes of the Indian Mutiny and Haiti in 1791.

Unfortunately, Raspail only cites "tradition" and religious faith as the bulwark that will defend France against the invasion of the Hindu "Ganges," as they are often referred to throughout the novel. All the excuses and rationalizations and expressions of self-flagellation uttered by the government, as Raspail assembles them and puts them into the mouths of various vacillating officials and media spokesmen, are just so many disconnected assertions that add up to no argument at all. It's eerily similar to what American conservatives are doing and saying today, who refuse to question the indoctrination of American schoolchildren from K1 up through university, administered by our Orwellian Department of Education, lest they be accused by the press and the intelligentsia of racism, bigotry, and intolerance.

FSM: How so?

Me: I'll let Raspail himself answer that question. Appended to the novel are several articles about the novel and Raspail, including an interview of him by the current American publisher. Raspail wrote a reappraisal of *Camp* for Le Figaro in 2004, "Fatherland Betrayed by the Republic." He cites the phenomenon of the French being "bludgeoned by the throbbing tom-tom of human rights, of 'the welcome to the outsider,' of the 'sharing' dear to our bishops, etc., framed by a whole repressive arsenal of laws known as 'anti-racist,' conditioned from early childhood with cultural and behavioral 'crossbreeding'…and with all the by-products of old Christian charity…." I can't think of a better description of what is happening in America as well in that regard.

One can't claim that the Christian ethos has been "hijacked" by liberal/left secularists, as the defenders and spokesmen of Islam aver about Islam. Like the ethos of Islam, it is likewise reducible to self-sacrifice and suicide, except that Islam is blatantly frank and open about its purpose and ends. In any contest between Mohammad and Christ, it is Mohammad who will be the victor. When Christ turns the other cheek and forgives Mohammad for not knowing what he's doing, Mohammad will lop off his head.

FSM: Are there any redeeming qualities to Raspail's novel?

Me: Yes, the fact that the European intellectual elite recognized that it was being attacked in the novel. That is the novel's only redeeming quality, from my perspective. The novel was not well-received in Europe because the race "metaphor" either eluded the critics or was taken literally by them. Surprisingly, it was more favorably received in the U.S. In France, it was largely vilified, dismissed or ignored. Now it's a kind of underground cult classic among European anti-jihadists. The bromides and banalities about how the West is guilty of impoverishing the Third World by keeping it dependent on charity and handouts, and so must tax itself to death to share more of its wealth to atone for the sin of being richer, and to open its borders to all comers, regardless of their agenda, echo every collectivist claim and altruist bromide and banality uttered by the news media, the universities, Lyndon Johnson, Jimmy Carter, the Clintons, and now by the Obama administration. The culpable are many and small. They are the champions of the Ganges, or of the Muslims.

Of course, the claim that the rich are rich and the middle class well-off because they "rob" or exploit the poor or the underclass is illogical. You can't become rich by robbing someone who has nothing to rob, you can't exploit someone who has no values to trade or who is ignorant of the value of what he and his ancestors have ignored for millennia and otherwise had no use for because he and his tribalist brethren chose to remain backward, primitive, and tribalist.

Raspail doesn't go into economics, doesn't defend capitalism, doesn't mention individual rights. While it's a badly written novel, *Camp* is still a compelling read, because it does show the consequences of ideas – or rather of the absence of ideas. By the end of the novel, southern France has become a Hindu colony, northern France is overthrown by the "underclasses," including Muslims, and the rest of Europe acts as a passive blotter for the phenomenon. Even Switzerland falls. The closest thing to the Islamic *jihad* is one mention of the Archbishop of Paris handing over Notre Dame to the Muslims to be turned into a mosque.

FSM: Going by your description of the novel, it sounds like it might be worth cracking open, but with all your caveats in mind. Is there a moral to the story?

Me: The chief moral to be drawn from *The Camp of the Saints* is that the West cannot absorb countless immigrants from Third World countries and cultures without establishing legally enforceable conditions for their coming to the West and settling in it. But such conditions are an anathema to the liberal/left philosophy of multiculturalism, diversity, "pluralism," and tolerance. This is especially important when those same immigrants come to it with no intention of assimilating themselves into Western culture or adopting any of its values, but rather to import their primitive culture intact and impose it on the West in the name of "diversity" or "religious freedom" or "tolerance." These are ideas of Western origin, and contain the seeds of suicide.

I doubt that Raspail ever made the connection between individual freedom, industrial civilization, and the wealth the West was able to produce because of them. It isn't evident at all in the novel or in his prefaces, articles, or interviews. He didn't note that the welfare state is a magnet for maggots and parasites, domestic or foreign-born, he failed to suggest that the welfare state, premier among collectivist institutions, must be abolished if any Western values are to be preserved and sustained. And by "welfare state" I mean also foreign aid to any and all countries that pull at America's altruist heart-strings, which countries usually spit on us and demand more, adopting a stance of moral superiority.

This is not the novel I would recommend to anyone to better grasp what has happened and is happening in Europe, and in slower motion here in the U.S., in the way of concessions and accommodations to the carriers of an alien, anti-life philosophy. Hordes of Hindu manqués are no better than mindless hordes of Huns, Muslims, Apaches, Chinese, Mexicans, Patagonians, or Caucasians. Or, as a distant friend of mine would call any one of them, but specifically Muslims, "not lovable normal human beings – but cultural vacuums, black holes of creativity and humanity, a tribe of nobodies, just the bloody vanguard foot soldiers representing a totalitarian mindset that has no sense of humor, no capacity for self-criticism and no respect for other people's views."

Well, I would say that a lack of a sense of humor is merely a venial sin of Islam's, not its cardinal offense, which is its refusal, indeed, its inherent inability, to "self-criticize." The creed forbids questions of any nature, which is why it cannot and will not respect other people's views. Muslims can't criticize it, nor kaffirs or non-Muslims without risking the charge of "hate speech." Not even Pope Benedict could get away with a circumspect criticism of it. It is forbidden. That explains its totalitarian nature. No one ever said that the face of Big Brother had to be a kindly one staring out from an INGSOC poster. He can also be wearing a Brooks Brothers suit and a turban staring out from an ISLAMSOC poster.

FSM: Thank you, Mr. Cline

* *The Camp of the Saints*, by Jean Raspail. 1973. Trans. Norman Shapiro. (Petoskey, MI: The Social Contract Press, 2007).

December 2010

The Ghouls of Grammatical Egalitarianism

Originally published in *The Social Critic*, November/December 1996, Vol. 1, No. 5

A small, innocuous-looking book appeared in bookstores recently, published under the auspices of the Association of American University Presses (AAUP), an organization which claims to be devoted to the dissemination of knowledge and scholarly research. Its title is *Guidelines for Bias-Free Writing*, by Marilyn Schwartz and the Task Force on Bias-Free Language (Bloomington: Indiana University Press, 1995). It is little more than 100 pages long, weighs less than a pound, yet its contents are more potent than the Oklahoma City bomb. Its ingredients are politically correct jargon, multiculturalism, and the phenomenon of what may be called "grammatical egalitarianism."

It is important to note at the start that the Association boasts a membership of 114 institutions, mostly university presses, but includes such diverse organizations as the National Academy Press, the National Gallery of Art, the Modern Language Association, the Russell Sage Foundation, and the J. Paul Getty Trust. Its membership includes all major American and Canadian universities, plus Oxford University Press and presses in Tokyo, South America, and Scandinavia. This is an organization with significant cultural clout.

What is "bias-free" writing? The *Guidelines'* definition of it is "writing free of discriminatory or disparaging language." It should be stressed that the object of *Guidelines'* concerns is not primarily racial slurs. The AAUP is not referring to the language to be found in the pathological hate literature published by the Ku Klux Klan, the Aryan Nation, or the Black Muslims, but to staid *university* publications. Its focus is common, inoffensive usage, and the implication throughout the book is that scholarly works that are not "sensitized" and "sanitized" may in the future be demoted to the rank of hate literature, and treated with the same disdain, regardless of their intellectual merit or significance.

The following is a short selection of terms, phrases and usages from *Guidelines*, found by its authors to be discriminatory, disparaging or otherwise "biased":

> *Man*, the singular pronoun *none* coupled with *his; girl, mother nature*, the alleged association of *he* and *she* with *good and bad* and *great and small; born-again, retard, idiot, redneck, city slicker, Siamese twins, Dutch treat, deprived, needy, underprivileged, well-dressed, ghetto, indigenous, tribe, teenager, juvenile* and

elderly. Also on its list of "offensive" terms are *able-bodied* and *intelligent,* which are considered discriminatory by implication and disparaging in any instance of comparison.

Guidelines includes the disclaimer, "there is no such thing as a truly bias-free language" and stresses that the advice it offers is only "that of white, North American (specifically U.S.), feminist publishing professionals." The Task Force, which is composed of 21 university press editors (two of them men), recommends euphemistic proxies for all of the terms on its "hit list."

> "Books that are on the cutting edge of scholarship," reads the AAUP Board of Directors' position statement, "should also be at the forefront in recognizing how language encodes prejudice. They should also be agents for change and the redress of past mistakes." By "prejudice" *Guidelines* means an operative hierarchy of values, not racist premises or gender "chauvinism." While the term "encodes" suggests that the authors of *Guidelines* regard the human mind as a kind of computer chip that must be sterilized before "correct" encoding can be applied (and who therefore imply that the mind is a mere passive receptor and mirror of its cultural environment), another statement deserves still closer scrutiny: "The term *normal* may legitimately refer to a statistical norm for human ability (such as 20/20 vision), but should usually be avoided in other contexts as…invidious."

If one sets as his standard of *normalcy* an individual who is in full possession of his mental faculties, who is not debilitated by disease or physical impairment, who is able to take responsibility for his own life, can think and act without special "accommodation," then by definition most people are normal, and any limitation in any of these criteria is a measure of subnormalcy.

In private conversation, one might say of another, "He's feebleminded." In public – e.g., in a "sanitized" book or in a speech – one may be allowed to say, "He's cognitively challenged," or "He's conceptually arrested," or "He's differently conscious." But assuming an absence of malice or cruel intent, the use of the adjective "feebleminded" represents a conclusion reached from an evaluation or a judgment of a person who, for whatever reason, chooses not to exercise his mind, and thereby renders himself comparable to a feebleminded person who has no choice in the range or depth of his thinking.

The same argument can be applied to any of the supposedly discriminatory or disparaging terms targeted by *Guidelines.* Suppose one said, "He's an idiot," or "He's a moron," or "He's a retard"; or was more inventive: "His mind is on crutches," or "His brain is in a wheelchair." Assuming that one has made an accurate observation and a just evaluation, the more terse or colorful one's descriptive prose, the more heinous one's act of disparagement. But, in fact, one is not mocking or disparaging idiots, morons, or non-ambulatory men: they are merely being used as referents of normalcy.

In essence, *Guidelines* advocates abolishing human comparison by prohibiting the identity of referents. In the foregoing example, one would be discouraged from expressing a judgment or evaluation of a person who has offered abundant evidence of his inability or unwillingness to think normally or to perform some task. Such a person is simply there, like a rock or a tree, beyond discrimination (in the strict, nonracial, nonsexist meaning of that word), beyond evaluation, beyond recognition. He is not incomparable; more precisely, he is *non-comparable*. To compare the inventor of the steam engine with a man who is unable to do simple math or boil a kettle of water without harming himself is, by egalitarian anti-standards, a grave breach of "social justice" and an unforgivable *faux pas.*

According to *Guidelines*, "[a]djectives such as *poor* and *unfortunate* have a similar [negatively connotative] effect and are patronizing, as are such epithets as *heroic* and *courageous*." Thus, if *Guidelines*' authors have their way, not only will it be considered a breach of egalitarian etiquette to make a distinction between heroism and cowardice, but it will not be permitted to establish distinctions between normalcy or abnormalcy by which to measure anyone's character, ability or physical condition.

There will be no such thing as normalcy or any hierarchy of values, or value-measurement, just whatever the slot machines of egalitarianism and multiculturalism happen to disgorge from an eclectic, random stew of humanoids. A genius and an idiot are not to be distinguished, discriminated, or even recognized; each is "differently abled" or "specially conscious," and no value may be placed on one over the other.

This is not the pursuit of "social justice," even if one could assign a benign intent to the concept. It is a formula for the manufacture of politically correct automatons.

Strictly speaking, measures of subnormalcy are *not* moral judgments. Neither are they absolute measures of one's potential for achievement. Helen Keller was both blind and deaf. John Steinmetz, the brilliant electrical engineer, was a hunchback. Toulouse-Lautrec, the painter, was a dwarf. Neither is gender an obstacle to achievement, nor is race, especially not in regards to intellectual accomplishment or to any field of productive work that entails a greater than average measure of mental labor. The numbers represented by women and individuals of other races or cultural backgrounds in this respect are so great that they do not represent exceptions to the rule – the rule *simply does not exist.*

(Parenthetically, the act of blacklisting supposedly disparaging terms is self-defeating. Readers will recall how quickly the first wave of politically correct euphemisms was met with disdainful humor. What occurred was the transfer of the intended evaluations or judgments from the banished terms to the euphemisms. The intent of the evaluations or judgments found a new mode of expression – with the added, stressed note of contempt for the euphemism itself, for its stumbling, awkward redundancy, for its ill-disguised role of shielding the subject of the euphemism from true identification or evaluation.)

Grammatical Egalitarianism

Webster's defines egalitarianism as "a belief in human equality, especially with respect to social, political and economic rights and privileges." *Grammatical egalitarianism* is the systematic culling of "offensive" words and phraseology from the English language and the substitution of innocuous or "preferred" argot, at the expense of clarity, economy and logic, for the sake of protecting the *feelings* of real or imagined "victims of such offending language.

In economics, egalitarianism is the philosophical root of antitrust laws and graduated taxation; in politics, of the welfare state and modern university admissions standards. If we treat the identification of individuals or of specific human conditions as "social" elements of some egalitarian ideal, then grammar has lagged behind economics and politics – until now. Grammatical egalitarianism would be employed to "catch up" by leveling people's conceptual and evaluative criteria, so that by law, etiquette or custom, no person can be distinguished from another, and to no one's advantage but the lowest common denominator's.

Perhaps the most troubling aspect of *Guidelines* is that its contents are not at all shocking ore revolutionary. The "guidelines" contained therein are already a matter of ubiquitous, if uneven, conformity in business, government and the news media. In its bibliography are listed more than a dozen other publications, by university and trade publishers alike, that serve as guides for "nonsexist" and "bias-free" writing. While this would imply that the AAUP Task Force's effort is redundant, perhaps merely a postscript to a culture-wide phenomenon, it is in fact much more. The welfare state introduced new meanings to such terms as *deprived, disabled,* and *handicapped.* As a politically correct metathesis, grammatical egalitarianism strives to purge language of *all* human distinctions and measures, regardless of their origin.

To illustrate the potential influence of *Guidelines*, imagine that a scholar whose field of study is American political history has, after years of work, finally completed his *magnum opus* on modern political trends. His thesis is that, with very few exceptions to the rule, the character and capabilities of political officeholders tend to diminish in direct proportion to the growth of statism. This scholar's work is being seriously considered for publication by a university press. In his manuscript, however, are several statements of questionable egalitarian taste, one of which, summarizing chapters of dry commentary and rigorously researched proofs, reads, "Modern politicians are moral and intellectual midgets, when compared with the moral and intellectual stature of the Founding Fathers."

His editor at the university press might feel compelled to ask the historian to rewrite that and other allegedly offensive sentences, or to substitute bland proxies for *midget* and other red-flagged terms. The scholar cannot use *dwarf,* or *cripple,* or any other term that, either as a simile or a metaphor, implies a subnormal human condition; yet subnormalcy is the point he wants to stress and the Founding Fathers are his measure of integrity and intellectual achievement. He harbors no ill feeling toward or prejudice against midgets, dwarfs or the handicapped; he was not even conscious of them when he wrote the sentence. He senses that he had been *expected* to be conscious of them, but he dismisses that thought as too fantastic. He consults a dictionary of etymology, and learns that *midget* is derived from a variety of long-dead languages, and that its original meaning was a gnat-like insect or sand fly, i.e., the word existed long before it was modified to name a human condition.

What can the scholar do? Should he try to rewrite the sentences? Find substitutions? Remove the sentences altogether? Work out some kind of compromise? Or take a stand and insist that his words remain unaltered?

The answer depends on a host of unknowns. If the scholar does not want to risk reducing his chances for publication – and his career as a historian would depend on publication – he may not want to take a stand for the sake of a few words. Furthermore, he cannot know whether his editor is a staunch advocate of "bias-free" writing; or is indifferent to the issue and so not likely to risk offending his managing editor and coworkers, who may be advocates; or is a loner who is contemptuous of "bias-free" writing, but who is certain that he would be voted down in an editorial meeting. And there is always the AAUP in the background, ready to reconsider the status of recalcitrant members who publish books whose texts "encode prejudice."

If the editor manages to push through the historian's "unsanitized" work, the publisher may be upbraided by the AAUP or subjected to other unknown pressures.

If the scholar caves in and accommodates the editor and publisher, he sets a precedent for himself and other publishers and writers. "See? Even the champion of liberty and enemy of collectivism had the decency to compromise. Why can't *you*?" And if the scholar takes a principled stand against having his work sanitized – if he does not wish to become an "agent" for a change he does not endorse, if he does not want to become a "redresser" of mistakes he either does not concede or had no role in – he will do so with the knowledge that he risks rejection of his work, for there are other, less troublesome authors willing to be published under almost any conditions.

This scenario depicts the conflict faced by an accomplished adult who presumably, in his formative years, could avail himself of the *Oxford English Dictionary*, *Roget's Thesaurus*, and *Webster's Synonyms and Antonyms* before large sections of these reference works were X'd out by grammatical egalitarianism and declared off-limits by his teachers. It is a dilemma in which many authors might soon find themselves, unless they are fortunate enough to have courageous publishers willing to place paramount value on an author's ideas and competency, and none on his capacity for obsequious thought orthodoxy.

In her 1972 essay "The Establishing of an Establishment," Ayn Rand notes that:

> Private cliques have always existed in the intellectual field, particularly in the arts, but they used to serve as checks and balances on one another, so that a nonconformist could enter the field and rise without the help of a clique. Today, the cliques are consolidated into an Establishment....Rule by unofficially privileged groups spreads a special kind of fear, like a slow poison injected into the culture. It is not fear of a specific ruler, but of the unknown power of anonymous cliques, which grows into a chronic fear of unknown enemies.*

The relevance of her remarks as regards grammatical egalitarianism should be apparent.

The Atomization of Concepts

To *atomize* a concept for the purpose of destroying or repressing it is to explode a term into its constituent parts, treat the constituents as wholes in and of themselves, and finally inhibit the rediscovery or usage of the atomized concept with cognitive barriers. Well-known among logicians as a "reductionist" fallacy, this process repeals the law of

Occam's Razor, which states that entities are not to be multiplied beyond necessity.

Guidelines, which devotes almost half of its page count to the subject of how to achieve "gender-inclusiveness" in writing, focuses on the terms *he* and *man*. Reading the recommendations in *Guidelines* on how to atomize these terms is, at times, amusing: "[I]n subjects and traditions of discourse where *he* has been universally employed and men are assumed to be present, it [*she*] may temporarily redress the traditional omission of women." And: "Using words like *mankind* and *man* to refer to men and women, while convenient shorthand, embodies bias and introduces that bias into our perceptions of history and self. Use of the masculine singular pronoun [*he*] to refer to all people is misleading and exclusive." Thus, the concept *man* must be atomized into numerous phantom concepts which are never reunited under that term again by their essential attributes.

If one consults the etymological source of the term *he* and remembers how it is used in the generic sense, one will see that it is derived mostly from an amalgam of Old German and Old English, and has come to be used so that it and its derivatives, such as *his*, refer to a person of either gender. The terms *man* and *men* have similar histories, and have been used accordingly since the Enlightenment.

What the feminists are really objecting to are these terms' secondary but unavoidable masculine connotations.

The only answer to their objection is that the terms *he* and *his* and *man* must refer to some abstraction, or to some personified image of a human being. And since one of the attributes of the male gender, virility or potency, has been metaphorically linked to the physical and mental behavior of the human race, for better or for worse, the personified image or abstraction naturally defaults to *man*. Unless one is willing to settle for a circus freak, or a hermaphrodite, or even an "it" as an alternative to *man* or *he*, there is no other term that performs the same task.

And why would the grammatical egalitarians wish to atomize the term *man*? For two reasons: First, discarding the term gives them the rationale and precedent to perform the same vivisection on other, less complex terms; second, the term *man* does not include, and certainly does not evoke the image of, any of their pets: the handicapped, racial minorities, the elderly, homosexuals, or women. The term *man* is an ennobling term; it does not admit ciphers who refuse to poke their heads out of their particular group or tribal shells. The concept is a reproach to the egalitarians, for they see nothing noble or glorified within themselves that correlates to the concept, and nothing in the concept that can be applied to themselves.

"Insensitivity to racial and ethnic identities," continues the AAUP position statement, "and to differences of religion, age, ability, and sexual orientation reinforces the conscious and unconscious attitudes that allow us too often to reproduce ignorance."

Both in the AAUP position statement, and in *Guidelines'* table of contents, are cited as victims of discrimination, disparagement and injustice almost every group that has benefited from governmental social or economic legislation: minorities, women, the elderly, the handicapped, and homosexuals. However, that grammatical egalitarianism is being sanctioned and promoted by a quasi-governmental organization is not a fundamental cause of the phenomenon. Subjectivist art usurped representational art as part of a cultural trend whose root cause was the disintegration of philosophy. It was private foundations and a coalescing art Establishment which over decades banished representational art from parks, museums and business offices. The National Endowment for the Arts (NEA) did not appear until long after the fact.

Similarly, objectivity and clarity in language have been under attack from academe for decades, as ambiguity and imprecision in language gradually became hallmarks of sophistication and wisdom among the pseudo-intelligentsia. It was only a matter of time before the sewer lines through which the universities have been spewing effluvia into the culture themselves became rotted. The proposed "homogenization" of language by grammatical egalitarianism is merely another feature of a wider phenomenon, with government nomenclature and subsidies abetting and accelerating the trend.

Thought Orthodoxy

Thought *orthodoxy* is not synonymous with thought *control.* There is no Federal Board of Language Usage to which publishers must submit their books and journals to be tested for discriminatory of disparaging language before they can be put on the market for sale to the public. However, while no *official* agency of control exists, there is a kind of interlocking directorate of semi-public institutions and organizations which accomplishes the same purpose by presenting a united front against freedom of expression and imposing orthodoxy on our culture's intellectual and literary pacesetters. "Say what you please, we're not censors!" proclaims the AAUP's unspoken credo. "But say it *our* way, or do not bother to say it." Short of overt government repression, I cannot imagine a more insidious form of thought control than this, which is to thrust independent minds of whatever professional suasion or degree of ability into a purgatory that is not quite freedom and not quite slavery.

The goal of the grammatical egalitarians is not to diminish our range of thought, but to *homogenize* it. To homogenize the contents of a mind, however, is to accomplish the same end: unquestioning, knee-jerk obedience to the authority of orthodoxy. Such a mind may be able to produce a "sanitized" book without prompting by the czars of g*oodthink*, but it would never venture to extend its range of thought. Instead of reducing the number of words available to people in an ever-shrinking Newspeak dictionary (as described in George Orwell's novel, *Nineteen Eighty-Four*), *Guidelines* and its proponents advocate swelling the number of "value neutral" euphemisms for the ostensible purpose of preserving the "self-esteem" of the beneficiaries of collectivism and altruism (and, indirectly, to preserve the "moral" aura of the welfare state by squelching any incipient criticism of it).**

What of young minds? Discussing the issue of reprinting old or classic texts or collections of historical and literary documents, *Guidelines* advises that "Educated readers generally understand that scholarly publishers may not revise the language in a reprinted text... *unless the text is intended for classroom use in the primary and secondary grades*." [Emphasis added.] Thus, an educated adult may be permitted to read unexpurgated, unsanitized reprints, because he will somehow know better than to be "prejudiced" by whatever "disparaging" language he may encounter. The minds of children and adolescents, however, must be homogenized before "encoding" sets in, and so it is permissible to tamper with old or classic texts.

In the scholar's case, the cognitive obstacle is fear – fear of recrimination from unknown powers and influences in the realm of publishing. In the school textbook case, the cognitive obstacle is *engineered* ignorance by schools in concert with the publishers of textbooks – a practice that has been unofficial policy in public schools for decades.

Ayn Rand concluded her 1972 essay, "Censorship: Local and Express" with a dedication to Jefferson's vow, inscribed in marble above his statue: "I have sworn...eternal hostility to every form of tyranny over the mind of man."*** She wondered how conservative members of the Supreme Court could bear to look at the Jefferson Memorial in light of their decisions. In 1996, the grammatical egalitarians are neither blind to the magnificence of the statue, nor deaf to the meaning of the words. They would prefer to see the statue and the words replaced with an NEA-financed androgynous hulk who humbly swears subservient deference to any random cipher who chances by.

Guidelines reflects almost every collectivist trend that has come to fruition over the past thirty years: gender conflict, egalitarianism, the elevation of mediocrity, the indulgence of the irrational as a right, and the theft of physical and spiritual wealth under the rubric of "social justice." The grammatical egalitarians have assigned themselves the task of concealing the destruction caused by these and other trends behind a wall of words designed to exclude reason, inquiry and truth. This wall is composed mostly of euphemistic, concept-destroying argot; lining the top of it is the barbed wire of envy and the broken glass of malice. The wall will remain intact for as long as men consider it their altruist duty neither to question its existence, nor to wonder what it hides, nor to speculate whether it is meant to protect or to imprison them.

Under the entry "The Aggrandizement of Mediocrity" in *Usage and Abusage*, the late lexicographer and grammarian Eric Partridge concluded a poignant commentary on the decline of standards in literature, the arts and language with the observation that "[a]nyone who believes in civilization must find it difficult to approve, and impossible to abet, one of the surest means of destroying it. To degrade language is finally to degrade civilization."**** Had he lived long enough, Partridge might have made the astonished observation that there exist those who do not believe in civilization, who both approve and abet its destruction, and who are dedicated to diminishing men's minds by degrading language as a means of finally degrading civilization, not by reason of ignorance or ineptitude, but as a conscious, informed policy.

* P. 168, in *Philosophy: Who Needs It*, Signet paperback, first published 1984

** See Orwell's "The Principles of Newspeak" in the Appendix following the conclusion of the novel (in virtually any English language edition). While it is a brilliant essay on the methodology of the deliberate epistemological stunting of minds, there is a distinct difference in goals between the grammatical egalitarians of today and the totalitarians of the novel. Ayn Rand rightly remarked that such a society as Orwell describes could not long survive even as a semi-industrialized one, chiefly because the minds that could make it function would perish from the direct or indirect use of force. And, there is another difference between the grammatical egalitarians' purpose and that of the minions of Big Brother, which is that the former wish to impose thought orthodoxy on everyone, while the latter imposed orthodox thought and language only on ruling Party members. Rulers who reduced their range of concepts to the parroting vocabulary of an autistic person would not be able to continue making and maintaining telescreens, helicopters or any other product of free, thinking minds, nor would they be able to indefinitely retain their power, as Orwell suggests such a dictatorship could, regardless of the degree of their brutality.

*** P. 188, in *Philosophy: Who Needs It*, Signet paperback, first published 1984.

**** Addenda, p. 379, *Usage and Abusage: A Guide to Good English.*
London, Hamish Hamilton, 1947. Reprinted in softcover by Penguin,
1981.

December 1996

The Ignoble Nobel Peace Prize

One searches in vain through the whole list of Nobel Peace Prize winners from 1901 to the present for a single laureate whose work measurably advanced the cause of peace. The term *peace* itself, as it is employed by the Nobel Committee, on the surface is wishful and ethereal. The Peace Prize has, as a rule, recognized peace efforts which have unfailingly come to naught. Why? The "peace" pined for is essentially a Kantian concept. It is disconnected from reality. Work for peace, urges the Committee, even if your efforts are spoiled by war and conflict. Peace is good for its own sake. Work for peace as though you wished it to become a maxim, a moral rule.

The "peace" sought after and rewarded by the Nobel Committee is an unconditional peace that admits no legitimate grounds for war or conflict — nor any rational grounds for peace or war. Alfred Nobel set the original terms for the Peace Prize in 1895 when he said that it should be given to "the person who shall have done the most or the best work for fraternity between nations, for the abolition or reduction of standing armies and for the holding and promotion of peace congresses." In 1895, Nobel might have had a different idea of a "fraternity between nations," which certainly could not have included the conquest or subjugation of one nation by another. Still, it is an altruistic statement of pacifism.

The Nobel Peace Prize discards the concept of the initiation of force by one country against another — or by one individual against another — as a criterion for evaluation, and substitutes an inverted moral judgment. The wishes of the initiator of force should be treated just as legitimate as the wishes of his victim. If the victim resists, war or conflict result. That is bad. Violence ensues. Ergo, the victim must compromise and cede some or all of the initiator's wishes, if there is to be any "peace."

Thus, for example, the continuing pressure on Israel to sacrifice its existence to the likes of Yassir Arafat, Hamas and other killers and predators. Or the pressure on the U.S. to not defend itself against its attackers, or to sign the Kyoto Treaty that would destroy what is left of its industrial base.

It is a premise shared by the Nobel Committee, and by most of the laureates, benign, disreputable, and indifferent alike. Thus the Prize's futility. It is, appropriately, a Kantian trophy of no consequence, a blue ribbon for good intentions. Thorbjoern Jagland, former Norwegian prime minister who chaired the five-member selection committee (elected to the committee by the Norwegian parliament), defended the committee's choice against charges that Obama had accomplished nothing to deserve the award.

"We are not awarding the prize for what may happen in the future but for what [Obama] has done in the previous year...We would hope this will enhance what he is trying to do."

Jagland also explained away the fact that Obama was nominated for the prize about two weeks into his presidency, before he had a chance to move on any item on his agenda.

"Some people say — and I understand it — 'Isn't it premature? Too early?' Well, I'd say then that it could be too late to respond three years from now," Thorbjoern Jagland, chairman of the Norwegian Nobel Committee, told the AP. "It is now that we have the opportunity to respond — all of us."

Jagland said the committee whittled down a record pool of 205 nominations and had "several candidates until the last minute," but it became more obvious that "we couldn't get around these deep changes that are taking place" under Obama.

Those promised "deep changes" — meaning, among other things, the virtual regimentation of the American economy — are what moved Jagland and his colleagues to nominate Obama based solely on his campaign rhetoric, before Obama had a chance to routinely retreat to the Rose Garden to enjoy a Marlboro. In short, they awarded him the Peace Prize before he had won the election. That's the Chicago way: pretend for legal reasons to solicit open bids for a government contract, while having already chosen who's going to get it.

A gold medallion and a sack of cash will recognize the unrealized "efforts" of an American president, Barack Obama, who, to date, has failed to keep any of his socialist promises to transform America into a European collectivist knock-off — though he has helped to lay the foundation of totalitarianism here. In tune with Obama's continuing campaign slogan, the Nobel committee awarded Obama the prize in the "hope" that he will indeed "change" the U.S. into something with which it and its fellow anti-American European manqués would be more comfortable: a whipped giant, chained to servitude and sacrifice for the sake of the global poor, the environment, "social justice," and other "global challenges."

The reaction to the announcement of Obama's Nobel Peace Prize win has been, to say the least, "polarized." Daniel Pipes notes that "the absurdity of the prize decision will hurt Obama politically in the United States, contrasting his role as international celebrity with his record devoid of accomplishments." The Taliban and other Islamic gangs and spokesmen also made the same observation, demanding, "Show us the money!"

Media Matters, the left-wing mouthpiece of liberals and Democrats, responded immediately to any and all criticism of Obama's win in a posting, "Still rooting against America: Right-wing media use Nobel Prize announcement as excuse to attack Obama," and included links to several "right-wingers'" statements about the Nobel decision. That no one should need an "excuse" to attack Obama is beyond the grasp of these collectivists. He has provided Americans with numerous *reasons*, not including his three dozen or so "czars."

Bloomberg News also provided links to reactions to the announcement, some of the statements indiscriminately witless with delight, others dour and disappointed. "It sets the seal on America's return to the heart of all the world's peoples," French President Nicholas Sarkozy wrote to Obama. Those questioning whether he deserved the prize included Fawzi Barhoum, a Hamas spokesman in the Gaza Strip. "There's a lot more that Obama needs to achieve for peace and for the Palestinian people in order to receive this award," Barhoum said in a telephone interview.

Iran also sputtered raspberries.

Ali Akbar Javanfekr, media aide to Iranian President Mahmoud Ahmadinejad told AFP: "We hope that this gives (Obama) the incentive to walk in the path of bringing justice to the world order…We are not upset and we hope that by receiving this prize he will start taking practical steps to remove injustice in the world."

Raising his voice to be heard over this noisy tug-of-war between Pecksniffian mental astaticism and Islamic nose-wrinkling Obama, ever ready to comment on anything, expressed surprise at winning the Peace Prize. However,

> To be honest, I do not feel that I deserve to be in the company of so many of the transformative figures who've been honored by this prize — men and women who've inspired me and inspired the entire world through their courageous pursuit of peace.

Translation: Why didn't Saul Alinsky win the Peace Prize? He transformed me! Besides, I really don't know who else has won it, except maybe Al Gore, and that Southern cracker, Jimmy Carter. I looked up the list of past winners, and can't even pronounce half their names.

True to the Nobel Committee's "party line" and explanations of why it awarded the Prize to a non-achiever, Obama noted:

> That is why I've said that I will accept this award as a call to action, a call for all nations and all peoples to confront the common challenges of the 21st century. These challenges won't all be met during my presidency, or even my lifetime. But I know these challenges can be met so long as it's recognized that they will not be met by one person or one nation alone.

This is true. All those "challenges" require the employment of force to effect the changes to bring the U.S. more into line with a collectivized and increasingly barbaric world.

This award — and the call to action that comes with it — does not belong simply to me or my administration; it belongs to all people around the world who have fought for justice and for peace. And most of all, it belongs to you, the men and women of America, who have dared to hope and have worked so hard to make our world a little better.

Such *faux* humility sounds more like an Oscar speech than an acknowledgement; one keeps imagining him clutching a statuette, with his eyes glazing over to keep back the tears.

But, no, thank you, Mr. President. You keep it. By the terms of the Nobel Committee, you earned it. To your everlasting ignominy.

October 2009

Hoary Old Chestnuts

"Ever tried going into St. Paul's and offering to re-write the Bible?"– Lily Pepper to George Pepper, married but sparring vaudevillians, in "Red Peppers, an Interlude with Music," from Noël Coward's *Tonight at 8:30* (1935)

I rarely bother to beat dead horses. God is a dead horse, although religion is not quite as dead as most atheists believe, because it is alive and snorting and being harnessed to contemporary American politics. That is religion's special danger; churches of all stripes and sects are enlisting their congregations in the army for various welfare state, environmentalist, and collectivist crusades. Their primary object is to resurrect the country's alleged "Christian" values and rid that "Holy Land" of the infidel, the atheist, and incidentally clean up the earth, stop global warming, and herd everyone into a welfare state corral. It is God's will, they say, to take care of the lame, halt and poor by impoverishing the healthy, the independent, and the industrious.

At least two presidential candidates earnestly want to recapture the land in the name of God: Mike Huckabee, uncharismatic Baptist preacher, and Mitt Romney, practicing Mormon, who said he wishes to banish atheists from the country. Neither questions the morality of the secular application of his altruist creed in any fundamental way: the welfare state. The other presidential candidates bring God into their rhetoric only when they think it prudent. Each wishes to subdue the kind of atheist who does not believe in the mystical benefits of collectivism and involuntary servitude, to indenture him to them against his will for the sake of "giving back" to the national community, and thereby create a legacy for the candidate of being the "savior" of the "public good" and promoter of "social justice."

In the book I discuss below, I encountered one unattributed statement that aptly sums up the character and mentality of each of the current crop of presidential hopefuls. In a revealing description of the many fantasies of Heinrich Himmler, chief of the SS and Gestapo, the author remarks: "But one of his characteristics was much more widely shared – his mind had not been encouraged to grow. Filled with information and opinion, he had no critical powers."

And he certainly harbored an animus for them, did not welcome them in others, and counted on their absence in others – from Hitler down to the German populace – to sustain his totalitarian powers of life and death. To exercise one's critical powers in Nazi Germany was to risk a death sentence. For all their blather about the need for undefined "change" and the value of dubiously boasted "experience," each of the presidential candidates wears that double stigma on his forehead – an absence of critical powers and the insidious hope that no one else possesses them, either.

But, I digress. A friend gave me a Christmas present, *The Portable Atheist: Essential Readings for the Nonbeliever,* selected and introduced throughout by Christopher Hitchens (Philadelphia: De Capo Press, 2007, 499 pp.), author of the notoriously successful bestseller, *God is Not Great,* which exhaustively recounts the evil of religion and the imbecility of the idea of God under his various aliases.

I should state here that I became an atheist at a very early age, when I questioned the credibility and existence of Santa Claus. That is, I could not accept as a truth or even as the remotest likelihood a being who could somehow fly through the air from the North Pole, pulled in a sleigh by eight tiny reindeer, the rumble seat top heavy with presents for every child on earth, circumnavigate the globe in one evening, and return to the Arctic undetected even by NORAD. I was aware that there were millions of children like myself around the world, and that not all of them could boast of working chimneys in their houses for Santa to squeeze into and shimmy down into what should have been roaring fires on cold winter nights. We didn't have a chimney, either.

Also, I had observed that the roofs of most houses were too small to accommodate eight reindeer, regardless of their size. Further, most of the brightly wrapped presents it was claimed he hauled in his sleigh came in manufacturers' packaging. So, given all these conclusions, and the evidence of my senses, belief was not an option. This fealty to reality prepared me to question the existence of the other fellow in a long beard but who preferred to traipse about the universe in sandals and a nightgown, performing magic tricks, and who was not nearly as jolly as Old Saint Nick.

In fact, I had concluded, God was about as mean-minded and conniving as Satan, or the Devil. I even had the sense that He and Satan were in cahoots and had struck a deal: If you can make 'em sin, Satan, you can have 'em. But I had not yet articulated that species of price fixing among competitors.

Had I been able to intelligibly formulate them then, questions lurked in my mind that I could have asked my nominally Catholic foster parents: "Did the companies give these toys to Santa Claus to pass out to children? Or did they outsource their manufacture to his own shop, where his elfin helpers assembled them? Did his sleigh have retractable wheels that allowed him to land on roofs in places where it didn't snow? How would he know I had been naughty or nice in the year, unless *you* told him?"

I did not suffer the expected trauma or disillusionment of having a childhood fantasy exploded.

You see where this was leading me: ultimately to comprehensive disbeliefs in not only Santa, but in tooth fairies, the Easter Bunny, Heaven (especially when I first saw a photograph of the Andromeda galaxy), Hell, Limbo, Purgatory, angels, Satan, saints, ghosts, goblins, and every other kind of supernatural entity. One by one, the spirits, idols, and otherworldly realms fell victim to my loyalty to reality. Logic, according to the *OED,* is "the science of reasoning, proof, thinking, or inference." More fundamentally, logic, wrote Ayn Rand, is "the art of non-contradictory identification," and "rests on the axiom that existence exists." (*The Ayn Rand Lexicon*) The purported, magical attributes of the beings and realms contradicted the evidence of my senses and abused my logical mind. End of argument.

Until I applied logic to religion itself, I innocently subscribed to the delusion that my "soul" was a kind of ectoplasmatic representation of my torso, and that my two tummy freckles were the marks of indelible sins, one of them presumably "original."

So, God, the master wizard cum bogeyman of them all, had ceased to be a moral adviser and a vengeful threat long before I entered high school, simply because I knew he was not and could not be real, no more real to me than the volitional brooms unleashed by Mickey Mouse in Walt Disney's *Fantasia.* (For many of the same reasons, I never developed a liking for the device of talking animals, either, animated or otherwise.)

And, while I refuse to argue with anyone about the existence or non-existence of God, Jahveh, Allah or any of the other one hundred and ninety late gods and deities listed in H.L. Mencken's "Memorial Service" (one of the shorter essays in *The Portable Atheist,* and anything but funereal in sentiment), and have always been reluctant to waste time composing a rebuttal to such an absurd idea (that is, anyone who still needed convincing that there was no God, may as well still believe in Santa Claus), it was a breath of fresh air to read forty-seven essays and chapter excerpts penned by writers endowed with critical powers and bedeviled enough by the issue to perform the task.

For an incorrigible atheist like myself, these essays are both edifying and amusing. They begin with Lucretius's (96-55 BC) "On the Nature of Things," a poem that scuttles belief in gods – and pre-Christian gods, no less – and ends with Ayaan Hirsi Ali's "How (and Why) I Became an Infidel," an account of how she left Islam, which she damns in its entirety, seeing nothing in it that lends itself to "reform" or "moderation," and refused to accept a substitute religion, as Christians apparently pressed her to do.

It is hard to choose the most illuminating essays in this collection. One thing a reader is sure to come away with after reading, for example, Elizabeth Anderson's "If God is Dead, Is Everything Permitted?" and Ibn Warraq's "The Koran: The Totalitarian Nature of Islam" and Sam Harris's "In the Shadow of God" is the knowledge that Christianity, Islam, and Judaism are all religions that were knocked together from various pre-history pagan and tribal lore and barbarisms, sewn into their separate textual quilts over millennia by plagiarists, monks, scholars, imaginative tongue-in-cheek scribes and anyone else who derived sanctimonious pleasure from putting one over on the ignorant and credulous, which, beginning with the collapse of the Roman Empire and ending with the Enlightenment, was just about everyone. (It was news to me, for example, that one could be burned at the stake for owning a Bible that was in one's local language; one was supposed to rely on clerical authority about what the Bible actually said, and not commit the sin of seeing it for oneself.)

The reader will also learn, if he did not already suspect it, that the Bible and Koran especially were works-in-progress for about 1,500 years, and underwent constant emendations, corrections, excisions, deletions, revisions, additions, fraudulent attributions, and mistranslations in order to make them conform to preferred dogma or to make them "relevant" to the angst of the era. Neither the Bible nor the Koran of a millennium ago would be recognizable by modern day Christians or Muslims.

Neither religion can claim to be original even as "revelation," that is, as a direct communication from God or Allah, for both cadged the practice of Bronze Age shamans, witch doctors and holy men, that the not-to-be-doubted-or-questioned "Word" was ideally received by persons eminently lacking in critical powers, such as the bandit Mohammed and that ambitious camp-follower and prototype anti-Semite, St. Paul, both of whom laid the groundwork for the future and ongoing prejudice against and persecution of Jews.

Speaking of Jews, Sam Harris, in his chapter "In the Shadow of God," from his book, *The End of Faith*, devotes many pages to their demonization by Christian doctrine and superstition (not that there is much of a difference between them).

> "But for sheer gothic absurdity nothing surpasses the medieval concern over *host desecration*, the punishment of which preoccupied pious Christians for centuries. The doctrine of transubstantiation was formally established in 1215 at the Fourth Lateran Council…and thereafter became the centerpiece of the Christian (now Catholic) faith….Henceforth, it was an indisputable fact of this world that the communion host is actually transformed at the Mass into the living body of Jesus Christ. After

this incredible dogma had been established, by mere recitation, to the satisfaction of everyone, Christians began to worry that these living wafers might be subjected to all manner of mistreatment, and even physical torture, at the hands of heretics and Jews. (One might wonder why *eating* the body of Jesus would be any less of a torment to him.) Could there be any doubt that the Jews would seek to harm the Son of God again [Christian dogma alleges that the Jews betrayed him because they did not believe he was the Messiah], knowing that his body was now readily accessible in the form of defenseless crackers? Historical accounts suggest that as many as three thousand Jews were murdered in response to a *single* allegation of this imaginary crime."

I laughed out loud when I reached "defenseless crackers." I recall kneeling at the communion railing and having that tasteless, cardboard-like wafer plopped onto my tongue, and then nearly choking on it while trying to swallow it (we were cautioned not to chew it; that would have been "disrespectful"!). It was shortly after my "first communion" that I began to associate the whole ritual with cannibalism by proxy. It made no sense and the idea and ritual of the Eucharist became repugnant to me.

(I also laughed out loud when I read a December 30th column by Jeremy Clarkson, "Unhand my patio heater, archbishop," in *The Sunday Times* (London), which ought to be included in a second volume of *The Portable Atheist*, in which he upbraids Rowan Williams, Archbishop of Canterbury, for being a daft, yeah-saying hypocrite.

"Then we must ask how much old Rowan really understands about the implications and causes of global warming. He thinks that taking a holiday in Florida and driving a Range Rover caused the flooding in Tewkesbury this summer. But then he also believes it's possible for a man to walk on water and feed a crowd of 5,000 with nothing more than a couple of sardines.")

Elizabeth Anderson's "If God is Dead" essay is one of the best indictments of the Bible that I have ever read. Posing the conundrum of why God (or Allah, or whomever) is considered to be the be-all and end-all of morality – originating morality and rewarding it and punishing its delinquency – she writes:

"Consider first God's moral character, as revealed in the Bible. He routinely punishes people for the sins of others. He punishes all mothers by condemning them to painful childbirth, for Eve's sin. He punishes all human beings by condemning them to labor, for

159

Adam's sin (Gen. 3:16-18). He regrets his creation, and in a fit of pique, commits genocide and ecocide by flooding the earth (Gen. 6:7). He hardens Pharaoh's heart against freeing the Israelites (Ex. 7:3), so as to provide the occasion for visiting plagues upon the Egyptians, who, as helpless subjects of a tyrant, had no part in Pharaoh's decision. (So much for respecting free will, the standard justification for the existence of evil in the world.)"

I am willing to bet that somewhere, at some time, some preacher or priest has latched onto the tale of the Great Flood and charged that it was God's punishment for the prehistorical episode of anthropogenic global warming, doubtless ascribing the phenomenon to all those atmosphere polluting, pre-industrial age fires that baked men's bread and kept them warm and allowed them to live. That, of course, would cast Al Gore in the role of prophet, a role to which he has proven to be amenable.

Anderson similarly exposes just about every book of the Bible and the enormity of its absurdity and of its obscenity as a handbook for ethical guidance, particularly because she demonstrates that God, as he is represented anywhere in the Bible, is a certified, psychopathic fruitcake. One cannot help but conclude that it is God who ought to be punished for his callous brutality, inhuman crimes, and blatantly irrational behavior.

Ibn Warraq's essay on the pitfalls, fabrications, contradictions, and immorality of Islam is long but absolutely priceless. On the subject of miracles, which Mohammed was not supposed to be able to perform because he was a mortal, for example, he relates how he miraculously fed thousands from a single lamb kid. Doubtless this tale was snitched from the one of Christ's feeding 5,000 people with his miracle of the loaves and fishes ("a couple of sardines") and adapted to inflate the Prophet's importance.

Unless I am mistaken, one point that none of the contributors to *The Portable Atheist* dwelt on was the fact that the three religions that have tortured the West for millennia – Judaism, Christianity, and Islam – share a common geographical origin: the Mideast. There might be some significance to that fact. That is where each creed's initial population of believers first appeared, grew in number, and spread to Europe and North Africa. Perhaps the climate contributed to the phenomena, or perhaps it was that combined with the nature of the region's topography, flora and fauna.

Another subject I would like to have seen discussed in greater depth was God's ostentation, coupled with his apparent shyness. He has appeared to no one but Moses, and that was as a burning bush. Both Christianity and Islam predict that he will make a Second Coming, announcing himself, or Christ announcing himself, with a "shout" (shouting *what?*). For a being who is omniscient, omnipotent, and frankly narcistic, he curiously finds it necessary to put on a big show of his Second Coming with blaring trumpets and resurrecting the dead and making everyone who ever existed (including Cro-Magnon men?) stand in line to hear his sentencing to heaven or hell – according to what is recorded in a big book. Well, why would this omniscient being need a written record? Would he not know who has been naughty or nice, and just be able to snap his fingers and send one on his predestined way without all the show-offy pageantry?

A few contributors only touched on the subject of what I would call God's self-esteem deficiency. Why does he need to be worshipped? Does he derive some joy in having people grovel before him in a quivering funk? Is he a sadist? Does he not feel complete unless someone is sweating bullets over the nature of his eternal reward or punishment? This nasty character and psychological profile of God differs in no fundamental from that of a common neighborhood bully or dictator, or even from that of any of the current presidential candidates.

These and other questions about God's psychological and moral makeup apparently have never occurred to theologians, priests, rabbis, mullahs and their ilk. But then again, these creatures have a vested interest in keeping God's profile and his purposes inscrutable and exempt from rational scrutiny. That makes these mortals accomplices in an unprecedented scam.

I end this foray into atheism and religion with a memorable quotation from an equally refreshing article in the April/May issue of *Free Inquiry*, Gerd Lüdemann's "What Really Happened? The Rise of Primitive Christianity, 30-70 C.E." In summing up the reasons why Christianity was able to spread through the untiring machinations of St. Paul of Tarsus, he concludes:

> "…[T]he success of Pauline Christianity reflected its accord with the spirit of the time. The world had become weary of thought. People wanted a convenient way to secure their immortality, and one of the most popular was by initiation into mysteries, two examples of which were baptism and the Lord's Supper. Let us be blunt: Paul's brand of Christianity – which became the movement's normative form – constituted a spiritual reaction against the Greek Enlightenment at the same time when state law, customs, and even forms of greeting came to be dominated by authoritarianism. The quintessential freedom of ancient Greece was throttled along with the constitutional spirit of the Roman state. Prerogative replaced research; faith substituted for knowledge; independence of the human spirit gave way to humble

subordination to an all-powerful deity in the sky; and slavish observance of divine commandments supplanted natural human morality. When Paul's work was done, the downfall of the vibrant, ancient culture that had grown up out of Hellenism was complete."

Substitute a few of the subjects in Lüdemann's lament, and it could very well be a description of our own time. And comical Lily and George Pepper, bickering and washed-up hoofers and purveyors of "hoary old chestnuts," might have been surprised had they gone into St. Paul's and offered to re-write the Bible.

It had been done many, many times before. Why not again? They would have been as qualified as anyone else to undertake the task. All they would have needed to come up with was new material, keeping it clean, fresh and fragrant.

January 2008

Hoary Old Chestnuts Encore

"**A**ll 'scriptural' pseudo-scholarship is a strenuous attempt to make things come out right and to square a circle," wrote Christopher Hitchens in his introduction to another essay in *The Portable Atheist,* Martin Gardner's "The Wandering Jew and the Second Coming."

In light of the recent release by the National Academy of Sciences of its "final" word on creationism and "intelligent design," *Science, Evolution and Creationism*, I thought it apropos to add some notes of my own that I made in the course of composing my January 3 commentary. This is not an exercise in beating a dead horse, as I denied wishing to do in "Hoary Old Chestnuts," but rather a brief anatomical examination of some of the corpse that is religion – or, as Hitchens might put it, the shedding of some light on why a circle cannot be squared.

For the longest time, when the news media reports on the latest clash over the teaching of evolution and creationism or "intelligent design," the reportage, especially in TV news, is usually accompanied by pictures or footage of various animals and natural phenomena, that is, by strictly *benign* images of things God purportedly "created" or "designed." These as a rule include zebras, polar bears, tigers, and other photogenic wildlife, together with vistas of the Rockies, of rivers, forests, and the like. Never in my experience have I seen in such coverage pictures of things like flies, locusts, mosquitoes, plague *bacilli*, rats, boll weevils, hornworms, and other destructive life forms, or the devastation caused by earthquakes, tsunamis, tornados, volcanic eruptions, droughts, and forest fires. Nor have I ever seen God credited with a pack of lions feasting on a downed wildebeest, or a polar bear ripping apart a seal, or a jaguar pouncing on a deer.

Nor have I ever seen God associated with living human skeletons, whether they are in Nazi death camps or in present day, famine-reduced Africa, nor the faces of emaciated children covered with flies or the deformed bodies of the inmates of state-run institutions in Eastern Europe.

All this is God's doing – or so the priests and mystics claim.

If all these images were employed in TV reportage – particularly images of plague bacilli, rats, locusts, mosquitoes and any other parasite that can destroy but play no other role in their destructiveness or in the preservation of anything but their own parasitical existence – the question might be asked: Why did God create them? An advocate of "intelligent" design or creationism cannot credibly defend their existence, except to assert they are all part of God's "plan." And what is that "plan"? The advocate can only answer one of two ways: that they are a punishment for man's disobedience or the like, or that the "plan" is inscrutable and beyond human comprehension. We do not even have the assurance that God will reveal the purpose of his "plan" when he stages his "Second Coming."

But either answer sends the argument beyond reason and beyond debate into the spinning wheels of circular argumentation. Reason and debate, however, are not the favorite means of communication of the mystics, but rather preaching and appeals to emotion and an insistence on belief in defiance of human epistemology and a way to sanctimoniously "flip off" metaphysics.

All those non-benign things and more presumably adhere to God's "plan," and are products of his "creativity" and "intelligent" designing. One might be tempted to ask: What's so "intelligent" about disease-carrying flies and mosquitoes? When man creates a new software program or vaccine, does he also concoct viruses or bacilli that would cripple the program or compromise the vaccine? No. But, God does, which is why I would characterize him as a psychopathic fruitcake.

Intelligence, however, is not a synonym for rationality. A villain can exercise intelligence. The key distinction between the terms is whether the intelligence is rational and pro-life, or irrational and anti-life. God, Allah, and all the other monotheistic supreme beings are in the same ward as Hannibal Lector.

When the theological notions of God's plan, his omniscience, and the notion of man's predestination encounter the concept of free will or volition, a multiple vehicle collision occurs from which only the concept of volition emerges unscathed.

If one possesses genuine volition, not only in regards to moral issues, but to everyday thinking and action, it would conflict with a supernatural "plan." However, if every one of those attributes is claimed to be God's "plan," then it cannot be free will or volition that one possesses.

If God is omniscient, it presupposes that he knows in advance everything one will think and do. Again, this cannot be free will.

The same logic applies to the notion of predestination. If one is predestined from birth in all one's thoughts and actions, then the concept of free will is superfluous. If one's life, actions and end are predetermined by God, then the concept of free will is meaningless and a sham. Further, on the premise of predestination, if one commits a sin or a crime, why would God hold one accountable, if the sin or crime were predetermined? And if one performed a good action, or had no immoral thoughts, how could one be given credit for it by God, and rewarded? The notion of predestination obviates the concepts of reward and punishment.

The concept of free will or volition cannot be reconciled with any divine power or attribute. Nor can reality "square" with the idea of a supreme being. Moreover, it is fruitless to claim that God created man and the universe, and then retired from the scene as an impartial observer. On that premise, what would have been the point of creating anything?

The National Academy of Sciences report, however, asserts that science and religion – that is, reality and faith, or facts and wishful thinking – are not necessarily natural antagonists. It claims that "attempts to pit science and religion against each other create controversy where none needs to exist." The presumably stellar panel that produced the NAS book, which concedes a place for the teaching of creationism and intelligent design in public schools, has reduced itself to the intellectual level of Rodney King. It effectively pleads, "Can't science and religion just get along?"

No. One must destroy the other. Reason, the foundation of science, must dislodge faith, whose foundation is the unreal, from its role as a moral or "spiritual" guide.

The same book, reports the *Times*, "also denounces the arguments for a form of creationism called intelligent design, calling them devoid of evidence, 'disproven' or 'simply false.'" "Science and religion are different ways of understanding the world," states the book.

One step forward, two steps back. That is a retreat borne of compromise. It is also an instance of what Ayn Rand called the "soul/body dichotomy." The panel members could not conceive of a metaphysics that did not admit the "disproven" and the "false," nor of a limitless, reason-governed epistemology that rejects the unprovable and the fanciful and maintains a recognition of and loyalty to reality.

> "In 1984 and again in 1999," reported the *Los Angeles Times* on January 4 in an article, "Evolution Book Sees No Science-Religion Gap," "the National Academy of Sciences, the nation's most eminent scientific organization, produced books on the evidence supporting the theory of evolution and arguing against the introduction of creationism or other religious alternatives in public school science classes." The 2008 report makes a fatal concession to religion, doubtless from political pressure from religious groups and perhaps also from a fear of "offending" those groups and consequently risking the Academy being embroiled a controversy it is reluctant to ignite, or more crucially, lacks the confidence it could argue and win.

But any concession by science to faith and mysticism means, ultimately, an abandonment of truth and reality. Faith and mysticism acquire the attribute of being "real," while the truths discovered by science are shunted to the realm of subjectivism, allowing, for example, million year old fossils to be offered by religionists as proof of God's "handiwork," and not of evolution.

In her January 6 review of Lee Harris's *The Suicide of Reason: Radical Islam's Threat to the Enlightenment* in *The New York Times*, Ayaan Hirsi Ali applauds the book but has this reservation:

> "Harris...fails to address the enemies of reason within the West: religion and the Romantic movement. It is out of rejection of religion that the Enlightenment emerged; Romanticism was a revolt against reason."

Romanticism or the Romantic movement was a cultural phenomenon spanning the end of the 18th century and well into the 19th. The *Britannica Concise Encyclopedia* aptly describes it as a movement which "emphasized the individual, the subjective, the irrational, the imaginative, the personal, the spontaneous, the emotional, the visionary, and the transcendental....Among its attitudes...was a general exaltation of emotion over reason and of the senses over intellect...."

> "Moral and cultural relativism (and their popular manifestation, multiculturalism)," observes Ali, "are the hallmarks of the Romantics. To argue that reason is the mother of the current mess the West is in is to miss the major impact this movement has had, first in the West and perhaps even more profoundly outside the West, particularly in Muslim lands."

She could just as well be speaking about Christianity and its votaries when she remarks,

> "Thus, it is not reason that accommodates and encourages the persistent segregation and tribalism of immigrant Muslim populations in the West. It is Romanticism. Multiculturalism and its moral relativism promote an idealization of tribal life and have shown themselves to be impervious to empirical criticism."

Western leaders – and I am thinking of intellectual leaders as well as political ones – writes Ali, "must allow reason to prevail over sentiment."

And that is not what the National Academy of Sciences has done. Although *Science, Evolution and Creationism* faults creationism – and by implication any species of mysticism, anti-reality, or anti-reason – within the same document it claims that science and religion can work together as partners.

Speaking of political leaders not allowing reason to prevail over sentiment, not many readers may be aware of Congressional House Resolution No. 888, referred to the House Committee on Oversight and Government Reform on December 18, 2007, whose full title is:

> "Affirming the rich spiritual and religious history of our Nation's founding and subsequent history and expressing support for designation of the first week in May as "American Religious History Week" for the appreciation of and education on America's history of religious faith."

I will shred this presumptuous and wholly erroneous nonsense in a future commentary. Thanks to Mel McGuire, who was responding to "Hoary Old Chestnuts," for bringing this perilous proposal to our attention.

In *The Portable Atheist,* one will read of numerous attempts by Christian and Islamic scholars and religious authorities to square their pet circles. It is thanks to the efficacy of reason that they have been found out.

Ibn Warraq's "The Koran" discusses not only the invention of the Koran and the development of Islam, but also the invention of Christianity, as well, for the two are intimately linked to each other and to Judaism. One thing that might be noted is that the fabricators of Christianity and Islam were dishonest. As Warraq demonstrates in his essay, they invented biographical accounts of the lives of Christ and Mohammed in order to patch over holes in their separate dogmas. These in turn over time became unverifiable myths rife with miracles, and the myths in turn were seized upon by believers who wished them to be true.

In the course of his exhaustive but excellent essay, Warraq makes a number of interesting observations.

> "Despite the fact that there were approximately sixty historians active during the first century of the Roman world, there is remarkably little corroboration of the Christian story of Jesus outside the Christian traditions. What there is, is very inconclusive and unhelpful – Josephus, Tacitus, Suetonius, the Younger Pliny."

> "The letters of [St.] Paul were written before Mark's Gospel, and yet rather surprisingly they do not mention many of the details of Jesus's life that we find in the Gospels; no allusions to Jesus's parents, or to the Virgin Birth, or to Jesus's place of birth; there is no mention of John the Baptist, Judas, nor to Peter's denial of his master. As G.A. Wells points out, 'they never refer to his trial before a Roman official [Pontius Pilate] nor to Jerusalem as the

place of his execution. They mention none of the miracles he is supposed to have worked...."

Warraq comments,

"Just as we find that the early Christians fabricated details of the life of Jesus in order to answer doctrinal points, so we find that Arab storytellers invented biographical material about Muhammad in order to explain difficult passages in the Koran." Later, he writes, "Where Christianity arose from a fusion of Judaic and Greco-Roman ideas, Islam arose from Talmudic Judaic, Syriac Christian, and indirectly, Greco-Roman ideas."

One will not hear that stated in any Sunday morning sermon or any Friday evening exhortation in a mosque.

I do not wish to make a career of arguing against God, religionists, creationism, and other supernatural fantasies. But, aside from *The Portable Atheist* and all the similar works cited in it, other books have been written that might be of interest to anyone fascinated by the subject. Dr. John A. Henderson alerted Rule of Reason to books he has written on God and religion and how they have had a deleterious effect on just about everyone, including politicians: *A Deity for the New Millennium, Fear, Faith, Fact, Fancy*, and the co-authored *Judging God.* His website is: www.johnhenderson-god.com. Mr. McGuire, cited above, also recommended Chris Rodda's *Liars for Jesus*, the first title of a projected trilogy on religion, excerpts of which can be read at

www.liarsforjesus.com.

I have not read these latter books, and so cannot endorse them, but if Dr. Henderson and Mr. McGuire were encouraged by my last commentary on the subject of religion, I cannot imagine there would be any serious objection to recommending them.

And that is as much as I plan to discuss religion for a long while.

January 2008

Reality Catches Up With Art

Readers old enough to remember their high school civics classes might recall an earlier expression of "multiculturalism" and "diversity" before these terms were ever coined, that America was a "mosaic" of races and cultures, not a "melting pot" of reason, freedom, and the rule of law. They may recall, with some distaste, their teachers expounding with sanctimony on the subject and their textbooks describing it in preacherly prose. Neither the teachers nor the textbooks, however, offered any guidance or advice about what would happen or what action to take if the elements of that "mosaic" proved to be inimical or hostile to each other and resulted in violent, destiny-defining clashes.

Move from the classroom to home and television. Fans of the four series of *Star Trek* will recall the "Prime Directive," a world "Federation" rule that forbade Enterprise crews from "interfering" with primitive alien cultures, no matter how barbaric and irrational they were. With very few exceptions in the episodes, this rule was strictly and conscientiously observed. Also stressed in the series was the notion of "toleration" of alien cultures and practices, no matter how impossibly "inhuman" they were portrayed. Those cultures were to remain "pure" and undisturbed, left alone to "evolve" on their own, if ever.

But what was the origin of these ideas? Long before the debut of *Star Trek* in the 1960's, they had filtered down from the modern philosophy taught in our universities to Hollywood, philosophy imported from Europe and tailored for American consumption and promulgation over the course of a century. The relativistic, anti-reason, subjectivist, anti-absolute, reality-denying contents of that philosophy, unopposed by even so much as a fillip of Aristotelian philosophy, helped to indoctrinate not only the writers of those and other television programs, but the culture in general. Then came multiculturalism, "diversity," and "tolerance," all shielded under the mantra of political correctness.

President George W. Bush may or may not have been a *Star Trek* fan, but the "Prime Directive" seems to be the foundation of his foreign policy. Islam, in his view, is a religion of peace "hijacked" by extremists and criminals, against whom we are waging (and losing) an unimaginably costly war. Islam, to him, is itself exempt from criticism or judgment. The true nature of the creed eludes him. The thematic similarities between the Koran and, say, Hitler's Mein Kampf, apparently are beyond his grasp. If Iraqis "democratically" vote themselves a theocratic government as repressive as Iran's, the West should not be judgmental, even though it is sacrificing blood and treasure to make it possible. "Tolerance" means adopting a policy of non-judgmentalism, and is the natural partner of the altruistic policy of "sacrifice."

We can, however, thank the *Star Trek: The Next Generation* for introducing and concretizing a new nemesis long before its real-life counterpart made itself known. This was the "The Borg," a ravenous, nomadic phenomenon bent on conquest through the destruction of civilizations and the absorption and forcible conversion of their inhabitants into ant-like ciphers with no volition of their own. Its collective by-word and warning was "Resistance is futile." The sole alternative to submission to it was death. Its goal was to erase all traces of individuality and values from men so they could better serve "the hive."

Islam (or submission) can be characterized as a real-life "Borg." Islam is a creed that demands unthinking, unreserved submission and obedience to the commands of a ghost, purportedly related by an angel (Gabriel) to a pedophilic barbarian-cum-prophet some fourteen centuries ago, and that encourages the conquest and absorption of secular Western societies under primitive Sharia law. Colonies of Muslims appeared and grew in the midst of those societies, in Europe, Canada, the United States, and other Western countries. They were an alien phenomena that first seemed as anomalously insular as the Amish and Hassidic Jews, but have begun to exhibit a virulence that would not otherwise have been noticed, acknowledged or even tolerated but for the emasculating effects of multiculturalism, diversity, and tolerance.

Then-chairman of the Council on American-Islamic Relations (CAIR), Omar Ahmad, told a gathering of California Muslims in July 1998 that "Islam isn't in America to be equal to any other faith, but to become dominant. The Koran...should be the highest authority in America, and Islam the only accepted religion on earth." If that ever came to pass, what would happen to the Declaration of Independence and the Constitution? Presumably they would suffer the fate of the Alexandrian Library in a Muslim campaign to cleanse men's minds.

Islamic spokesmen and activists belligerently demand, first, "toleration" of their irrationalism, and then the cessation of any form of criticism of the creed that could be deemed or defined as blasphemy, offense, or "hate crime." On the premise that Islam cannot be "reformed" into a less hostile, non-aggressive creed without destroying it — a task that would in fact render it as "benign" as that of the Amish, and no longer "Islam," once its homicidal commandments were expunged from the Koran — what has been the overall Western response to its demands, which are absolute and non-negotiable? Why is the West retreating from the threat of conquest? Why does resistance to Islam appear to be "futile"?

Let us examine some incidents in which Western values, especially freedom of speech, have been challenged and confronted by Islam, and all but abandoned by the West.

In Britain, during the height of the Danish Mohammed cartoon uproar, the police covertly photographed demonstrators in London who carried placards that promised or advocated death for the cartoonists and anyone who "insulted" Mohammed. These demonstrators, however, if they are arrested, will not be charged with inciting murder or violence against individuals, but with "hate crimes." Conversely, anyone expressing a position on Islam that Muslims could claim to be offensive, may also be charged with a "hate crime."

The notion of "hate" crime subverts the whole idea of criminal responsibility, in addition to making mere thought a crime. On one hand, the concept treats an emotion as a crime and grants it legal, prosecutable legitimacy. Since all emotions are based on conscious or subconscious evaluations, or thought, an emotion can manifest itself in some form of objectionable expression (which could be rational or irrational) in oral or printed form.

On the other hand, the notion of "hate" crime grants legal legitimacy to the purported victim's claim of offense, wounded pride, or other emotion-based response to any criticism of the victim's "beliefs," including a sense of jeopardy caused by the "offending" expression.

How easy it will be to shift the definition of a "hate crime" from an inflammatory placard or a shouted imprecation during a demonstration to include an article, essay or book! Are Western judiciaries ready to strike down hate crime laws? No. They are rapidly endorsing their introduction into Western legal systems.

Most Western newspapers demurred reprinting the Danish cartoons out of "sensitivity" to Muslim religious values (although Muslim-run newspapers and news services feel no such constraint when depicting Jews, President Bush, or Western values). The staffs of several American and European university papers were fired or penalized for printing the cartoons. In Minnesota, a professor of geography at Century College was censored by her school's administration for posting some of the cartoons on the bulletin board of her department, even after she hid them from random sight.

Several Mideast editors ran some of the cartoons, not out of sympathy with freedom of speech, doubt about the veracity of Mohammed, or to defy their governments, but simply to show other Muslims what the uproar was about. They were arrested, or dismissed, and their papers closed. One editor in Yemen (a U.S. "ally") faces the death penalty.

Europe is reaping the perilous harvest of its decades-long experiment in multiculturalism and tolerance of the irrational, and there is no reason to think that the endemic Muslim violence there will not be emulated in the U.S. Many European countries, especially France, are experiencing a spike in gang rapes of "unveiled" European and "apostate" Mideast women by Muslim men and teens as a form of jihad. European politicians, artists and writers who have spoken out against the dangers of Islamofascism or who have been critical of Islam must have police protection. Many Muslim sections of European cities are "no go" areas to the police. A Turkish Muslim proclaimed in 2003 that Paris, Rome and Madrid were now components of the Islamic world because so many mosques have been erected in those capitals.

It can't happen here? American Muslims are not "into" jihadist behavior? Daniel Pipes has on his site logged dozens of instances of "mini-jihadi" in the U.S. committed by resident Muslims, the most recent being the attempted murder on March 3rd of students on the campus of the University of North Carolina by an Iranian immigrant who drove an SUV into a crowded pedestrian zone with the intent of killing as many Americans as he could. Mohammed Reza Taheri-azar, age 22, was the quintessential "moderate," Western-educated Muslim and model student (majoring in philosophy and psychology) who before his action displayed no overt signs of hostility towards his adopted country. His statements, after his arrest, comprise the kind of anti-American rant one can find on jihadist websites or in al-Quada videotapes.

Pipes is understandably perplexed by the event, and writes that Taheri-azar was "not some low-life, not homicidal, not psychotic, but a conscientious student and amiable person." He reaches some wrong conclusions and offers an irrelevant solution. Muslims, he writes, should develop "a moderate, modern, and good-neighborly version of Islam that rejects radical Islam, jihad, and the subordination of 'infidels.'" However, the term "radical Islam" is redundant. Remove jihad and the subordination of infidels from Islam, and there is no Islam. The problem is the creed, just as it is with Christians who attack abortion clinics or murder doctors, and with environmentalists who torch car dealerships or attack animal research labs.

The idea of "non-interference" ala *Star Trek* is evidence of multiculturalism's influence in the general culture. It, diversity and "tolerance" combine to close the door to rational discussion and persuasion in every detail. It renders helpless law enforcement to deal with the irrational, barbaric ethics and practices of Islam. Muslims can get away with their irrationality under the protection of multiculturalist "tolerance." Any proposal or move to dilute Islam's "purity" as practiced by Muslims triggers claims of Islamophobia or apostasy or even racism, not only by Muslim spokesmen, but by many Westerners, as well (such as Hollywood). From the Islamic perspective, "tolerance" is a unilateral policy to be benefited only by Muslims, while "multiculturalism" or "diversity" certainly is not on the Islamic agenda of global or even American or European conquest.

Only two choices are open to the West: submission to Islam by means of a totalitarian repression of free thought and expression imposed by Western and especially by American authorities; or an assertion of the Western values of reason and individual rights and of their superiority over any species of mysticism, and a declaration of true war against Iran, Syria, and Saudi Arabia. The alternative is to experience the degradation of progressive subservience or "tolerated" dhimmitude in deference to the "Borg."

March 2006

§   The End   §